Anne Hutchinson

Leaders of the Colonial Era

Lord Baltimore

Benjamin Banneker

William Bradford

Benjamin Franklin

Anne Hutchinson

Cotton Mather

William Penn

John Smith

Miles Standish

Peter Stuyvesant

A Woman Who Stood Up for Her Beliefs

On a bitterly cold November day in 1637, a solitary woman stood before the 40 men who made up the Massachusetts General Court in the barn-like building that served as the town of Cambridge's courthouse and only church. Despite the frigid weather, the drafty wood meetinghouse was packed with spectators. They had come to watch the trial of Mistress Anne Hutchinson, a 46-year-old midwife, spiritual advisor, and mother of 12, who was destined to go down in history as colonial America's first female religious leader.

Seated at a long table in the center of the meetinghouse was Hutchinson's chief judge and prosecutor, the governor of the young Massachusetts Bay Colony, John Winthrop. "Mrs. Hutchinson," he declared sternly, "you are called here as one of those that have troubled the peace of the commonwealth and the churches." She had done so, Winthrop explained, by leading religious meetings in her Boston home for men and women, even though the popular gatherings had been officially condemned as "a thing not tolerable nor comely [pleasing] in the sight of God nor fitting for your sex." Moreover, Winthrop charged, Hutchinson had slandered the colony's Puritan clergy and their preaching, a grave offense in a society in which church and state were intertwined. Should Hutchinson refuse to acknowledge her misdeeds and repent, the governor warned ominously, "then the court may take such course that you may trouble us no further." Winthrop's harsh words and demeanor were clearly intended to frighten the defendant into submission. The governor, however, would soon discover that Anne Hutchinson was not a woman to be so easily intimidated.

Over the course of the next two days, Hutchinson—who was denied a lawyer—defended herself brilliantly, parrying Winthrop and Deputy Governor Thomas Dudley's relentless questions with a devastating mixture of scriptural expertise, logic, and nerve. Hutchinson's powerful intellect, keen knowledge of the Bible, and remarkable self-assurance were not enough to sway the court, however. In fact, they almost certainly did more injury than good to Anne's cause. At a time when women were barred from holding public office, voting, attending college, preaching, or even speaking aloud in church, and were expected to be unfailingly obedient and modest, Hutchinson's bold courtroom performance won her few supporters among the male magistrates and ministers who ruled Massachusetts. By debating her male "betters" instead of meekly submitting to their correction, Hutchinson had "stepped out of [her] place" as a godly Puritan woman, in the words of one clergyman who testified against her at the trial. Even more incriminating, she had dared to instruct men as well as women at her heavily attended religious meetings and by publicly belittling the ministry and their preaching. By the close of the trial, all but three of the 40 members of the General Court had

Anne Hutchinson defied the clergy of the Massachusetts Bay Colony and was banished from the settlement. Refusing to alter her beliefs, Hutchinson left the colony in order to pursue religious freedom.

concluded that "Mistress Hutchinson" was a woman "unfit for our society," and should "be banished out of our liberties and imprisoned till she be sent away."

Anne Hutchinson's unwillingness to remain within the boundaries of traditional gender roles clearly dismayed Massachusetts' Puritan leadership. Nonetheless, most historians agree that it was Hutchinson's unorthodox religious opinions, particularly regarding the central issue of salvation (the deliverance from sin and its divine penalties), rather than her "masculine" behavior, which they found most worrisome. Today, the difference between Hutchinson's views on salvation and those of her orthodox opponents would probably strike most people as theological hairsplitting. (Theology is the systematic study of religion and of the nature of religious truth.) For Hutchinson, Winthrop, and most of their fellow colonists, however, all aspects of their Puritan faith were taken extremely seriously. "It would be difficult to overestimate the importance of religion in the New England world," contends historian Marilyn Westerkamp in her essay "Anne Hutchinson, the Puritan Patriarchs, and the Power of the Spirit." Massachusetts Bay's Puritan founders never doubted there was just one correct path to God and that believers had a sacred duty to silence any person who refused to stick to that path, especially if he or she was in a position to lead others astray as well. Consequently, Winthrop and the rest of the colony's orthodox elite were determined to stop Hutchinson's "erroneous" religious opinions from spreading any further among the people of Massachusetts Bay than already had occurred through her popular Boston meetings. Likewise, Hutchinson hoped that by publicly condemning ministers who held what she viewed as serious misconceptions about the salvation process, she could end the preachers' "corrupting" spiritual influence over the Puritan community and lead New Englanders back to the one "true" faith.

Hutchinson paid a heavy price for remaining stubbornly faithful to her religious convictions. Five years after being forced out of Massachusetts Bay, she was brutally murdered in the New York wilderness during an Indian raid. Yet Anne Hutchinson's story did not end with her death. Published accounts of her dramatic trial before the Massachusetts General Court in November 1637 and of a second hearing before her Boston church for heresy a few months later made Hutchinson one of the most famous women in colonial history. Over the centuries, she would come to be remembered as a pioneer of American religious freedom and a founding mother of feminism. Although most historians today agree that she was neither, Anne Hutchinson was an exceptionally courageous and independent-minded woman who dared to assume a leadership role and stand up for her beliefs in an authoritarian, male-dominated society.

2

The Reverend Marbury's Daughter

Anne Marbury Hutchinson was born in eastern England in the town of Alford toward the end of the long reign of Queen Elizabeth I (1558–1603). Located in the county of Lincolnshire, Alford is about five miles (8 km) from the North Sea coast and 140 miles (225 km) northeast of London. At the time of Anne's birth in 1591, just 500 people lived there. Arranged around a central market square, the entire town consisted of a few dozen thatched-roof houses, one church, and several large common fields. Individual families farmed these unfenced fields in long strips as part of a traditional "open field" system of agriculture that dated back to the early Middle Ages.

Little is known about Anne's childhood in Alford, including even the exact date of her birth. According to church records, Anne's parents, Francis and Bridget Dryden Marbury, had her baptized on July 20, 1591. Because infants in Elizabethan England were typically baptized when they were two or three days old, historians speculate that Anne was born on July 17 or 18. The new infant had three older sisters at home, including two half sisters, whose mother was Francis Marbury's first wife, Elizabeth. After Elizabeth's death in 1585, Francis married Bridget Dryden. Both Bridget and Francis came from socially prominent families that were part of the landed gentry. The English landed gentry were typically small landowners, who rented their property out to tenant farmers rather than farming it themselves. About 10 years younger than Francis, Bridget was a skilled midwife, meaning that she helped to deliver babies. Francis and Bridget had two other children together— a daughter, born in 1588, and a son, who died in infancy—before Anne's arrival in 1591.

FRANCIS MARBURY TAKES ON THE ANGLICAN CHURCH

Anne's intensely religious and outspoken father, Francis Marbury, was destined to have a deep influence on her life. Nearly six decades before Anne stood up to the Puritan leaders of Massachusetts Bay, Francis boldly took on the leadership of England's state church, the Anglican Church, or the Church of England, as it was also known.

Francis was born in 1555—three years before Elizabeth I inherited the throne from her older sister, Mary—and he grew up about 35 miles (56 km) from Alford, in the town of Lincoln. His father, William Marbury, was a prosperous landowner. Although he was not rich, William was sufficiently well off to provide his son with the luxury of a college education. In Elizabethan times, a small and privileged group of young men attended college. No young women attended, since females were barred from England's two universities,

Cambridge and Oxford. When he was 17 years old, Francis enrolled at Cambridge to prepare for a career in the church. After four years of study, including instruction in Greek and Hebrew so that he could read the Bible in its original languages, he was ordained a minister of the Church of England.

The Anglican Church had become England's state church in 1534 during the reign of Elizabeth's father, Henry VIII. (A state or "established" church is a church that has been officially endorsed by a country's government.) Today, Henry VIII is most famous for having had six wives, two of whom he divorced. Henry's decision to found the Anglican Church as England's state religious institution had its roots in his first divorce, from his Spanish-born queen, Catherine of Aragon. Henry wanted to end the marriage in order to wed his young mistress, Anne Boleyn. As was true of almost every other European country at the time, England's state church in the early 1600s was the Roman Catholic Church, headed by the pope in Rome. Henry needed the pope's permission to legally annul (dissolve) his first marriage and take a new wife. In those days, popes could almost always be counted on to go along with monarchs in such matters. When Henry asked Pope Clement VII for an annulment, however, to the king's dismay, the pope put him off, saying he needed more time to consider the request. In truth, Clement was afraid of angering Catherine's powerful nephew and champion, the Holy Roman Emperor, Charles V. Fed up with Clement's foot dragging, Henry pushed England's national legislative body, Parliament, to denounce the pope's legal authority over English Christians. Then, after ordering England's senior clergyman, the archbishop of Canterbury, to annul his marriage to Catherine in January 1533, Henry defiantly married. The following year, when Pope Clement threatened to expel him from the Roman Catholic Church unless he renounced his second marriage, Henry broke completely with Rome by establishing the Anglican Church with himself as its supreme leader.

When Pope Clement VII was hesitant to annul King Henry VIII's marriage to Catherine of Aragon, the English monarch created the Church of England and declared himself its supreme leader. With his first marriage now deemed to be invalid, King Henry was free to marry Anne Boleyn (*above*).

Henry's argument with the pope and the Catholic Church was based on politics rather than fundamental differences in religious belief. Consequently, the king left the teachings and rituals of

England's new state church largely unchanged following his formal split with Rome in 1534. After Henry's death in 1547, however, his son and successor, Edward VI, began introducing Protestant ideas and practices into the Anglican Church, including allowing priests to marry and ending the use of Latin in religious services. Protestantism had its roots in the Reformation, a major religious movement that began in Western Europe in the early 1500s. The Reformation's chief leaders, including the German priest generally considered to have ignited the movement, Martin Luther, believed that some of the Catholic Church's practices and doctrines (main principles) had strayed from the Bible's teachings and needed to be reformed. They were particularly disturbed by Rome's growing emphasis on the ability of Christians to win salvation (God's forgiveness and deliverance from sin) through good deeds, including donating money to the Catholic Church. In contrast, Protestants argued that people could be saved only by their faith in Jesus Christ and not by their good "works" (actions). They also insisted that the Bible, rather than any human being, including even the pope, was the one true spiritual authority for Christians. In time, Luther and other Protestant leaders on the European continent gave up trying to reform the Catholic Church from within and founded their own churches.

During the short reign of Edward VI's successor and ardently Catholic half-sister, Mary, Protestantism briefly lost its foothold in England when Mary once again made Roman Catholicism her kingdom's established religion. After Elizabeth I inherited the throne from Mary in 1558, she immediately reinstated the Anglican Church, with herself as its head, and re-introduced most of Edward's Protestant reforms. Some English Protestants, however, were dissatisfied with the scope of Elizabeth's reforms of the state church. They believed that her reforms did not go far enough.

One of Queen Elizabeth's most outspoken religious critics was young Francis Marbury. Francis's insistence that the Anglican Church was in need of further reform got him into serious trouble with his clerical superiors shortly after he left Cambridge for his first ministerial assignment in the town of Northampton, in central England. Marbury's main complaint with England's state church centered on the quality of its bishops. (In the Anglican and Roman Catholic churches, bishops are high-ranking clergymen who are responsible for the spiritual well-being and administration of a certain diocese or region within a country.) Far too many Anglican bishops had been promoted to their posts for political reasons rather than their deep knowledge of the Scriptures or spiritual faith, Marbury believed. Week after week, the idealistic 22-year-old hammered away at the Anglican Church's unqualified bishops from his Northampton pulpit. Finally, the Anglican authorities had had enough. Determined to make an example of the young firebrand, they stripped Marbury of his Northampton post and sent him to jail for several months for slandering the church leadership. Not in the least deterred, Marbury headed straight back to Northampton upon his release from prison and began publicly attacking the Anglican bishopry again. This so incensed church authorities that, in November 1578, Francis was arrested and hauled off to London to stand trial before the Court of High Commission, England's supreme ecclesiastical (church) court.

MARBURY PAYS A HEAVY PRICE FOR HIS OUTSPOKENNESS

The presiding judge at Marbury's ecclesiastical trial, the powerful Bishop of London, John Aylmer, was known for his harsh treatment of ministers who dared to criticize the Anglican Church or its leadership. Francis, however, was not about to let himself be intimidated by Aylmer. Across England, Anglican bishops had recklessly endangered the spiritual health of their flocks by filling their dioceses' pulpits with poorly educated and trained ministers, he declared. "The Bishops of

London and Peterborrow and all the Bishops in England are guilty of the death of as many souls as have perished by the ignorance of the Ministers of their making whom they knew to be unable," Francis accused. Infuriated by Marbury's insolence, Bishop Aylmer sentenced him to two years in London's Marshalsea prison for badmouthing the clergy. Seemingly unfazed by this harsh sentence, Marbury was as defiant as ever in his closing words to the court: "I am to go whither [to what place] it pleases God, but remember God's judgments. You do me open wrong. I pray God forgive you."

When Marbury was finally released from Marshalsea in 1580, the Anglican leadership decided to give the 25-year-old one more chance. At a time when only about a third of the Anglican clergy had attended college, Francis's four years of study at Cambridge undoubtedly worked in his favor. Shortly after leaving prison, Marbury was offered the post of assistant minister at St. Wilfrid's church in Alford, the country town where Anne would be born about a decade later. In addition to his responsibilities at St. Wilfrid's, Francis was also hired as headmaster of the Queen Elizabeth Free Grammar School, located on the church's second floor. At the grammar school, Marbury taught Latin, Greek, and arithmetic to an all-male student body, ranging in age from about 10 to 14. As was true of all public schools in sixteenth-century England, girls were barred from attending Queen Elizabeth's School. Since it was generally assumed that a woman's proper place was in the home, caring for her husband and children, most Elizabethans looked on formal schooling as a waste of time for girls.

Marbury spent 10 relatively quiet years in Alford as a minister and schoolmaster. Then, shortly before Anne's birth in 1591, Francis's high principles and rebellious spirit got him into trouble again. In his sermons at St. Wilfrid's, Marbury increasingly returned to his old theme of corrupt and incompetent bishops. He even went so far as to denounce the erring Anglican leaders as "self-seeking soul murderers" who cared more for their own careers than for the spiritual well-being of their flocks. Marbury's impertinence outraged William Wickham, Bishop of the Diocese of Lincoln, to which St. Wilfrid's belonged. Accusing Marbury of being an "impudent Puritan" as well as a slanderer, Wickham barred him from preaching in the Lincoln Diocese and placed him under house arrest.

As harsh as Francis's punishment may have been, if he had not firmly denied Wickham's accusation that he was a Puritan, it would almost certainly have been far worse. By 1590, the Puritans were the largest and most influential group among the Anglican Church's various Protestant critics, and many of their leaders were sentenced to long jail terms during Elizabeth's reign. Puritans got their name from their determination to cleanse or "purify" Anglicanism of all shreds of "popish" (Roman Catholic) ceremony, ritual, and church ornamentation, including statues and pictures of saints and stained glass windows. Puritans also criticized the hierarchy of the Anglican Church as overly Catholic. They maintained that individual congregations should be the primary source of authority in the church, and not bishops. Queen Elizabeth wanted to keep the Puritans strictly in check both because she genuinely liked the old rites and traditions, and because the would-be reformers were demanding an end to all royal influence over the church.

FRANCIS GIVES HIS DAUGHTER AN UNUSUAL EDUCATION

Francis Marbury's house arrest lasted for three years, ending when Anne was about 2½ years old. Anne's biographers disagree as to exactly when Marbury was allowed to return to his ministerial career. According to historian Emery Battis, Francis was silenced—in other words, barred from preaching—in the Lincoln Diocese throughout Anne's childhood and early adolescence. Stripped of his ministerial

WOMEN IN SIXTEENTH- AND SEVENTEENTH-CENTURY ENGLAND

Throughout Anne Hutchinson's lifetime, all English females, unless they entered a religious convent, were expected to marry, usually by the time they were 21 or 22 years old. It was generally assumed that women were the "weaker sex," inferior to men in their intellect, physical stamina, and even in their moral character. A woman's proper sphere was home and hearth, and caring for her husband and children was her chief calling in life. Women were supposed to always have a male protector, with their husband assuming that role once they left their father's home to marry. If they were orphaned or widowed, then another male relation such as a brother, uncle, or grown son was expected to look after them. These patriarchal attitudes remained the norm in English society even during Elizabeth I's long reign, despite the high regard in which most of her subjects, male and female alike, held their accomplished and dynamic ruler.

As a potential heir to the British throne, young Elizabeth had received a demanding and well-rounded education from a series of highly qualified tutors, but she was the rare exception among women of her place and time. Shut out of grammar schools as well as England's two universities, Cambridge and Oxford, Elizabeth's female compatriots were forced to pick up whatever book learning they could at home, which for poor girls was typically none at all. In families of slightly better standing, daughters were sometimes taught the rudiments of reading, generally by studying the Bible. In addition to being taught to read, young ladies of noble heritage also often received instruction in music and foreign languages such as Latin or French from private tutors.

duties, Francis had plenty of time to focus on his growing brood of children, and particularly on their education.

The fact that Anne's university-educated father was able and willing to devote himself to his children's education was an enormous advantage for the bright and inquisitive girl. Formal schooling outside of the home was not an option for Anne or any other females of her era in England or throughout most of Europe. To improve Anne and her siblings' reading skills, while also developing their religious knowledge and faith, Marbury assigned his children long passages in the Bible and in English author John Foxe's *Book of Martyrs*. One of the most popular books in Elizabethan England, the *Book of Martyrs* was first published in 1563, five years after Elizabeth inherited the throne from her fanatically Catholic half sister, Mary I. In his work, Foxe described in gory detail the sufferings of the nearly 300 Englishmen and women who were burned at the stake during Mary's reign for refusing to denounce their Protestant beliefs. Elizabeth was so taken by Foxe's sensational account of England's Protestant martyrs that she insisted that a copy of the book be put in every Anglican Church in her kingdom.

In addition to the Bible and the *Book of Martyrs*, the Marbury children's other main textbook was a highly unusual one: a detailed record of their father's hearing before the Anglican Court of High Commission in 1578 for slandering the bishopry. Francis himself was the author of the account, which portrayed him as a courageous Christian hero and Bishop Aylmer as his arrogant and unprincipled persecutor. Marbury's trial for badmouthing his Anglican superiors took place 13 years before Anne's birth and more than a half century before the Puritan leaders of Massachusetts Bay tried her on similar charges. Nonetheless, because Francis made his account of the 1578 trial one of the central textbooks of her home schooling curriculum, Anne's outlook and character could hardly help but be shaped by this dramatic event in her father's life. It is impossible to know exactly what lessons Anne took from Francis's biting version of his church trial. But her biographer Eve LaPlante believes that Anne's close study of the transcript "left an abiding mark on her." Most significantly for Anne's eventual role as America's first female religious rebel, Francis's account of his lively battle of words with church leaders whom he viewed as his moral and intellectual inferiors encouraged in Anne "a willingness to question and even to show contempt for authority," writes LaPlante.

LONDON

In 1605, when Anne was 14, Francis Marbury was offered a new ministerial post 140 miles (225.3 km) from Alford in London. By this time, a decade and a half had passed since his previous run-in with Anglican authorities, and his old enemy, Bishop Aylmer, was long dead. The current Bishop of London, Richard Vaughan, was considerably more open-minded than Aylmer regarding the church's Protestant critics, as long as they were not followers of Puritanism. Probably the single most important factor in the willingness of the Anglican leadership to forgive and forget Marbury's troublesome past, however, was the severe shortage of ministers that the church faced in 1605, particularly in England's largest city, London.

The Anglican Church's shortfall of ministers had its roots in the strong anti-Puritan bias of King James I, who succeeded his cousin Elizabeth I to the throne in March 1603. The chief reason for James's intense dislike of the Puritans seems to have been their opposition to the doctrine of the divine right of kings, a principle that he passionately supported. Largely ignored by Elizabeth I, the divine right of kings was an extremely autocratic religious and political concept. It said that monarchs received their right to rule directly from God and were accountable to Him alone for their actions. As part of his

Born during her father's house arrest, Anne spent her earliest years being tutored by him. The Marbury children studied the Bible and read John Foxe's *Book of Martyrs*. Illustrated with woodcut prints, the *Book of Martyrs* contains stories of 300 men and women, including Sir John Oldcastle (*above*), who were burned at the stake for their Protestant beliefs.

crusade against the Puritans, James I removed some 300 staunchly Puritan ministers from office for refusing to sign an oath that they believed all of the Anglican Church's practices followed the teachings of the Bible. Whatever Francis Marbury's past faults may have been, at least he had always vehemently denied being a Puritan.

In the fall of 1605, Francis and Bridget Marbury packed up their nine children and household belongings and moved into the rectory at Francis's new church, St. Martin in the Vintry. (A rectory is the official residence provided by an Anglican parish for its minister or rector.) The rectory and church were located just north of the Thames River and a short walk from the Tower of London, the famous medieval fortress and prison. To 14-year-old Anne, who had spent her entire life in a small country town, her new neighborhood in the bustling heart of one of the world's biggest and most cosmopolitan cities must have seemed enormously exciting.

Little is known about Anne or the rest of the Marbury family's years in London. It seems likely, however, that Francis decided to hold his tongue about corrupt and incompetent bishops after moving to the royal capital, since he was given two other churches to oversee in addition to his large St. Martin in the Vintry parish between 1607 and 1610. According to some accounts, under Bridget Marbury's tutelage, Anne became a skilled midwife during her time in London, even assisting her mother during the births of a baby sister and two baby brothers between 1606, when she was just 15, and 1610.

In February 1611, Anne and her family suffered a terrible blow when Francis Marbury died suddenly at the age of 55. Fortunately for his grief-stricken wife and children, however, Francis had inherited a sizable sum of money from his father, meaning they were able to continue living in reasonable comfort despite the loss of his ministerial salary. Anne, who at the time of her father's death was the oldest of the 12 Marbury children still at home, stuck by her bereaved mother's side for the next year and a half. Then, on August 9, 1612, a few weeks after her 21st birthday, she married a childhood friend from Alford, William Hutchinson, in a simple ceremony at St. Mary Woolnoth Church in London. A short time later, Anne moved back with her new husband to her birth town to begin a new and challenging chapter in her life as a housewife, mother, midwife, and religious teacher.

3

Mistress Hutchinson

Anne's new husband, William Hutchinson, came from one of Alford's most prosperous families. Five years older than his bride, William was a successful cloth merchant like his father, Edward. Although the Hutchinsons had plenty of money, unlike Anne's family, they did not belong to the gentry. A few years before Anne and William's marriage in 1612, Edward had tried to talk royal officials into awarding his family a coat of arms. Because the Hutchinsons' wealth was still relatively new and rooted in trade instead of inherited land, the traditional source of the gentry's high social status, his request was rejected.

ANNE'S PROSPEROUS LIFESTYLE

William Hutchinson lacked his wife's high social standing, but his success as a merchant would have allowed the newlyweds to enjoy a privileged lifestyle, at least by the standards of little Alford. Bricks and lumber were scarce in Alford and throughout most of rural Lincolnshire at that time. Consequently, despite their wealth, the couple's home would have featured a timber frame with humble "wattle and daub" walls composed of straw, twigs, mud, and animal hair, like every other house in Alford in 1612. Still, even if the exterior of the couple's home was far from elegant, given William's substantial income, they could easily have afforded to build and maintain one of their community's largest and most comfortable residences. Historians do not know just how many rooms the Hutchinsons' house contained. It seems likely, however, that it had at least 10, making it five times the size of the typical seventeenth-century rural English home. Edward Hutchinson's Alford home, which was described in detail in a probate inventory taken after his death in 1632, had eleven rooms, including four bedchambers, two parlors, and two butteries or walk-in pantries. (A probate inventory is a court-ordered record of a deceased individual's personal property.)

As was the custom, Edward Hutchinson's probate inventory included a detailed list of his livestock, stored crops, and farming equipment as well as of each object found in his house at the time of his death, including pots and pans and furniture. Unfortunately for Anne's biographers, no record of her and William's household items exists. Historians speculate, however, that the couple would have owned many of the same kinds of luxury items as William's father. According to Edward Hutchinson's probate inventory, these included fine carpets, books, imported china, silver spoons, a massive oak cupboard, a wooden bathtub, and a four-poster bed with a goose-feather mattress—a sharp contrast to the thin straw pallets on which most Alford residents slept.

MOTHER, HOUSEWIFE, AND MIDWIFE

About nine months after her wedding, Anne gave birth to her first child, a boy. Anne and William named their infant son Edward, in honor of William's father, and had him baptized at St. Wilfrid's Church on June 28, 1613. Over the next 21 years, Anne would give birth about every 18 months. In all, she and William had 15 children, including seven boys and eight girls. Today, 15 children sounds like an exceptionally large family. But the Hutchinsons' big brood was not all that unusual by the standards of the time. In seventeenth-century England, women of childbearing age (approximately ages 15 to 44) gave birth to a child on an average of every two years. Anne herself was one of 15 children, and William had 9 siblings. What was unusual about Anne's brood was not its size but the children's physical hardiness. All of Anne and William's children managed to survive infancy at a time when nearly one in two babies in England died before reaching the age of 3, most of them from infectious diseases such as small pox or typhoid.

In addition to caring for her numerous children, Anne was responsible for a variety of demanding housekeeping duties. Among these were cooking meals for her family, baking bread, churning butter, cleaning, sewing, mending, washing clothing, hauling water, tending the kitchen garden, and helping to care for the livestock, including horses, cows, chickens, and a large herd of sheep. Yet despite her daunting workload, Anne was fortunate compared with many of her neighbors. Unlike most of her fellow townswomen, Anne did not have to rely solely on her older children to assist her with her many household responsibilities. As William's mercantile business continued to grow and prosper, the couple was able to hire several farmhands and house servants. In addition, two unmarried female relatives of William moved in with the Hutchinsons to help Anne care for her home and children.

Having servants and relatives to assist her with housekeeping and child care allowed Anne the luxury of pursuing other interests outside of her home. She decided to put the training she had received from her mother as a folk healer and midwife to good use in her

In addition to her household and family duties, Hutchinson also served as a midwife and provided medical advice and care to the local residents of Alford. Hutchinson was often called upon whenever a woman went into labor. Above, a fifteenth-century engraving of a midwife at work.

community. Soon, she became known throughout Alford for her expertise in preparing herbal cures for many common ailments, including fevers, coughs, and indigestion. Anne also relied on her knowledge of herbal medicine in her work as a midwife. For example, she treated her patients with homemade ointments or syrups concocted from betony and horehound to reduce labor pains and columbine to speed a slow delivery.

In seventeenth-century England, midwives were among the most valued and highly regarded members of their community. Physicians seldom monitored labor or delivered babies in those days. This was particularly true in rural areas, where medical doctors were few and far between. Like Anne, most midwifes lacked any formal training, instead learning their craft from older, more experienced midwifes and through hands-on experience. Nevertheless, not just anyone could be a midwife in England during Anne's lifetime. Midwifes had to be awarded a special license from the bishop before they could practice in their communities. To obtain the license, a prospective midwife had to provide the bishop with several character references and sign an oath of professional conduct. The midwife's religious character was of particular concern to the Anglican leadership. That is because midwives were expected to perform emergency baptisms on dying infants in the absence of a minister. Any women caught practicing midwifery without a license from the bishop could be tried in an Ecclesiastical Court and fined. Before assisting at births in her hometown, Anne would have had to obtain a license from the Bishop of the Diocese of Lincoln, the diocese to which Alford belonged.

When Anne Hutchinson was called to an expectant mother's home to oversee her labor and delivery, she could count on having plenty of company—all of it female. Childbirth was an important social ritual for women, in which female relatives, neighbors, and friends came together under the midwife's supervision to help the mother-to-be. Every bit as important as the practical assistance the women offered to the midwife was the emotional support they provided to the expectant mother. Until the development of modern obstetrical care in the nineteenth and early twentieth centuries, giving birth was a dangerous undertaking. (Obstetrics is the branch of medicine devoted to childbirth and care of the new mother.) Death during or soon after childbirth was common before the introduction of antibiotics, sterile practices, and advanced

ANNE BRADSTREET

North America's first notable poet—and the first female author to be published in England's American colonies—was Anne Dudley Bradstreet (1612–1672). Anne and her husband, Simon Bradstreet, were devout Puritans who immigrated to Massachusetts Bay from England in 1630 as part of a large group of Puritan colonists led by John Winthrop. Anne came from a wealthy family with an unusually enlightened attitude toward female education. During her childhood, Bradstreet was encouraged by her parents to read widely and received private tutoring in literature and several languages. After she and Simon settled in Massachusetts, Anne began writing poetry in her spare time. Published female authors were rare in seventeenth-century England and unheard of in the colonies. Consequently, Anne never imagined that any of her writings would appear in print. Her husband and brother-in-law, however, so admired her work that they secretly arranged to have a collection of Anne's poems published in London in 1650, under the title *The Tenth Muse, Lately Sprung Up in America*.

One of Anne Bradstreet's best-known poems, "Before the Birth of One of Her Children," concerns her dread of dying in childbirth, a fear that she shared with many other women of her era. The mother of eight, Anne wrote the poem as a farewell note to Simon toward the end of one of her pregnancies. In the event that she died in childbirth, Anne wanted her husband to know the depth of her affection for him.

"Before the Birth of One of Her Children"
All things within this fading world hath end,

surgical techniques. According to some estimates, as many as 1 in 50 women lost their lives as a result of complications from childbirth in seventeenth-century England. "Childbirth fever," a serious bacterial

Adversity doth still our joys attend;
No ties so strong, no friends so dear and sweet,
But with death's parting blow are sure to meet.
The sentence past is most irrevocable,
A common thing, yet oh, inevitable.
How soon, my Dear, death may my steps attend,
How soon't may be thy lot to lose thy friend,
We both are ignorant, yet love bids me
These farewell lines to recommend to thee,
That when the knot's untied that made us one,
I may seem thine, who in effect am none.
And if I see not half my days that's due,
What nature would, God grant to yours and you;
The many faults that well you know I have
Let be interred in my oblivious grave;
If any worth or virtue were in me,
Let that live freshly in thy memory
And when thou feel'st no grief, as I no harmes,
Yet love thy dead, who long lay in thine arms,
And when thy loss shall be repaid with gains
Look to my little babes, my dear remains.
And if thou love thyself, or loved'st me,
These O protect from stepdame's injury.
And if chance to thine eyes shall bring this verse,
With some sad sighs honor my absent hearse;
And kiss this paper for thy dear love's sake,
Who with salt tears this last farewell did take.

infection of the genital tract, was a particularly common killer of new mothers in the days before the connection between disease-causing germs and cleanliness and hygiene was understood.

RELIGIOUS TEACHER

According to contemporary accounts, at some point after moving back to Alford, Anne somehow found time in her hectic schedule to take on yet another role: that of religious teacher and adviser to her fellow townswomen. Anne's new role as an informal spiritual instructor to the female members of her community was probably linked to her part-time career as a midwife. With the specter of death always hanging over childbirth, many women turned to the comfort and hope provided by their religious beliefs to help them face the trauma of labor and delivery. Some historians have suggested that Anne first began offering religious guidance to her Alford neighbors at childbirth gatherings, by leading her anxious patients and their attendants in prayer and scriptural readings.

Eventually, Anne began holding regular religious meetings for her female friends and neighbors in her own home. She quickly assumed a leadership position at the private gatherings, directing discussions of readings from the Bible, and offering her own interpretations of difficult or unclear passages. Scriptural analysis was something for which Hutchinson was uniquely qualified because of the first-rate religious education she had received from her father when she was growing up. Anne's deep command of the Bible combined with her natural charisma and self-confidence won her a loyal following among the devout women of Alford. Many years later, her listeners still vividly recalled Anne's informative and insightful lectures on the Scriptures, particularly the epistles (letters) of the Apostle Paul and the book of Revelation.

In a later era, Anne Hutchinson might very well have chosen to pursue a career in the ministry. During her lifetime, however, women were closed out of the established ministry, just as they were from all of the other "learned professions." (In seventeenth-century England, the so-called learned professions were those careers that traditionally required an advanced education, including theology, medicine, and law.) No Christian church formally ordained female ministers until the mid-nineteenth century, when a handful of Protestant denominations, including the Unitarian, began accepting women into the ministry. The Anglican Church ordained its first female priests in the late twentieth century. Women were not completely barred from assuming positions of religious leadership in the Anglican community, however. Devout women were permitted to provide instruction in the Scriptures to other women within the privacy of their own homes, as Anne was doing with her all-female Bible study meetings. Yet the idea of a woman offering religious instruction to men along with women, even within the privacy of her own home, was offensive to the Anglican leadership, and for a woman to preach in church was out of the question. To justify the exclusion of women from the pulpit, church leaders typically pointed to the first letter of the Apostle Paul to the Christians of Corinth, Greece. In his letter, Paul instructed the Corinthians that "Women should be silent in the churches. For they are not permitted to speak, but should be subordinate, as the law also says. If there is anything they desire to know, let them ask their husbands at home. For it is shameful for a woman to speak in church." (I Corinthians 14:34-35)

ANNE DISCOVERS PURITANISM AND THE REVEREND JOHN COTTON

Sometime after marrying William Hutchinson and moving back to Alford, Anne began to develop a strong interest in Puritanism. Little is known about the clergymen who presided over St. Wilfrid's during the two decades between 1612, when Anne wed William, and 1634, when she and her family left Alford for the Massachusetts Bay colony. It is clear, however, that Anne's growing attraction to Puritan ideas and practices was not grounded in anything she was hearing from the pulpit of her hometown's one and only church. Years later, after she had settled in Massachusetts Bay, Hutchinson would recall

FEMALE "LAY MINISTERS" IN SEVENTEENTH-CENTURY ENGLAND

Although strictly barred from preaching in church, a handful of "non-conforming"—unorthodox—English women acted as "lay" preachers in the seventeenth-century. (A "lay" preacher is someone who is not a member of the regular clergy.) The Anglican leadership strongly disapproved of these unordained female preachers, both for their boldness in preaching before men as well as women and their unorthodox spiritual views. Many of the female lay preachers of seventeenth-century England claimed to be prophets. They believed that God had given them a special gift that allowed them to reveal and predict His future plans for individuals and nations. One of these female lay preachers and prophets, an unnamed woman from the small town of Ely, about 60 miles (96.5 km) south of Alford, managed to catch Anne Hutchinson's attention. Years later, after Anne had immigrated to Massachusetts Bay, she reportedly praised this anonymous "woman of Ely" as "a woman of a thousand, hardly any like her." Whether Anne admired the woman of Ely for her unconventional religious views or for her daring in preaching before a mixed audience of men and women is unclear. For the timing being, however, Anne would make no effort to expand her own role as a religious teacher beyond the female members of her community

being "much troubled by the orthodox stand" of St. Wilfrid's Anglican vicar (minister). Historians cannot say with any certainty exactly when or why Anne turned Puritan after returning to Alford, despite the strictly orthodox preaching she would have heard Sunday after Sunday at St. Wilfrid's. Yet most scholars assume that the source of her unconventional religious beliefs was the same Puritan minister who would eventually inspire her to abandon her birth land for the wilds of New England: the Reverend John Cotton of Boston, a major port city about 25 miles (40.2 km) south of Alford.

"It is not known when Mrs. Hutchinson first heard Cotton preach, nor how long a period passed before she completely accepted his views," writes Emery Battis. It is likely, however, that she first became aware of the popular and charismatic vicar of Boston's St. Botolph's Church through the communication network that grew up around her hometown's regular market days. As one of Lincolnshire County's approximately 35 official market towns, Alford had the legal right to host weekly outdoor markets in the town center for surrounding communities. On Alford's designated market day of Tuesday, farmers, craftspeople, and merchants flocked into town from nearby villages and farms to sell their wares and purchase items they lacked the time, desire, or expertise to produce for themselves. Hutchinson's biographer Selma Williams describes Alford's bustling weekly markets:

> Mixing, mingling, and thronging there were local townspeople and farmers from outlying areas, who, letting their horses rest from the one-to-three-hour ride while they unloaded and loaded their carts and wagons, tittle-tattled and talked all the while. Thus, amid the selling, buying or bartering of meat, fish (the North Sea was just six miles away), vegetables, fruit, grain, household utensils, and new and used clothing, Anne could easily pick up the latest news, views, and gossip.

Because Alford's role as a market town made it a hub for news, before Anne even had an opportunity to make the 25-mile journey to Boston to hear Cotton preach in person, she undoubtedly knew a great deal about the dynamic and brilliant young minister.

Born in 1584 in the town of Derby in Derbyshire County, John Cotton was just seven years older than Anne Hutchinson.

It is likely that the biggest influence on Hutchinson's Puritan beliefs was John Cotton, the minister of nearby Boston. Although she had to travel a great distance to hear his sermons, Hutchinson was drawn to his speaking ability and distinctive theological views. His teachings would later lead her to adopt even more radical theological attitudes regarding salvation than Cotton held.

His remarkable natural intelligence and deep love of learning were obvious from a very early age. By the time he was 13, John had already been admitted to Trinity College of Cambridge University. He would remain there for the next 15 years, establishing a reputation as one of the university's most talented and dedicated scholars. After earning his Bachelor of Arts degree in 1603 at the tender age of 17, Cotton went on to earn a Master of Arts in 1606. Immediately after receiving his master's degree, he was appointed as a tutor at Cambridge's Emmanuel College, where he rapidly moved up through the ranks to the position of head lecturer. During this period, Cotton experienced a spiritual awakening after hearing a sermon by the Puritan minister and theologian Richard Sibbes, and he converted to Puritanism. Deciding that he had a calling to reform the Church of England from within as a minister, Cotton began studying for a Bachelor of Divinity degree at Emmanuel College. After five years of intensive coursework in theology, disputation (debate), and Hebrew, Cotton was granted his third and final degree from Cambridge in 1613.

In July 1612, six months before he officially received his Bachelor of Divinity degree and one month before Anne returned to Alford as William Hutchinson's bride, John Cotton was offered the vicarage of St. Botolph's Church in Boston. Since it was one of England's biggest parishes, St. Botolph was a prize assignment for a newly ordained cleric such as Cotton. Despite his lack of clerical experience, it is easy to see why the congregation of St. Botolph's wanted Cotton as their minister. (Although bishops generally appointed vicars to the various parishes under their supervision, the Anglican leadership permitted a small number of churches, including St. Botolph's, to select their own ministers.) Not only was Cotton's educational training highly impressive, but he was also an exceptionally powerful and talented public speaker. His voice, wrote one admirer, "had in it a very awful [awe inspiring] majesty." Another contemporary glow-ingly described Cotton as "a man of great parts for his learning, elo-quent and well-spoken."

Once settled in the pulpit of St. Botolph's, Cotton more than lived up to his reputation as a skillful and inspiring orator. So many people flocked to hear the young minister that he began delivering six ser-mons a week, including a second Sunday sermon, morning sermons on Wednesdays and Fridays, and afternoon lectures on Saturday and Thursdays, Boston's market day. Although the majority of his audi-ences were members of the Boston community, some of Cotton's most fervent admirers were willing to travel substantial distances to listen to him preach. Among this particularly dedicated group was Anne Hutchinson. Writes Michael Winship in his book *The Times and Trials of Anne Hutchinson*: "William Hutchinson's business would certainly have taken him to Boston on market days, and Anne might have accompanied him to hear the famous Cotton preaching, or she might have gone on her own. Determined Puritans would travel many miles along the deeply rutted and at times almost impassable roads of England to hear their favorite preachers, and we know that Anne admired Cotton greatly."

Historians cannot say with certainty how often Anne made the nearly 50-mile (80.4-km) round-trip between Alford and Boston, which probably would have taken her a full three days to complete. Yet in light of what is known about the depth of Anne's devotion to Cotton by 1634, when she uprooted her family to follow him across the Atlantic to Massachusetts, it seems likely that she made the long trip to St. Botolph's as often as her hectic schedule allowed. While a substantial portion of Cotton's large and enthusiastic following may have been drawn more to his masterful speaking style and erudi-tion (learnedness) than to his unorthodox religious views, such was clearly not the case with Anne Hutchinson. Cotton's particular brand of Puritanism was to have an enormous influence on Anne, even though in the end, she would take his religious ideas in bold new directions that he had never intended.

4

A Crisis of Faith

The Puritans earned their name from their determination to purify the Anglican Church of all Roman Catholic rituals and ornamentation. Yet Anne Hutchinson was drawn to the movement by something more than merely a dislike of "popish" rites and practices. Anne's attraction to Puritanism was based on its teachings regarding God, humankind, and the nature of salvation, particularly as interpreted by her clerical idol, the Reverend John Cotton.

PURITAN THEOLOGY AND THE QUESTION OF SALVATION

Puritan theology differed from the central religious teachings of the Anglican Church and most other Protestant denominations in a number of ways. Most significantly, Puritans believed in predestination, a harsh concept first developed by the sixteenth-century religious reformer John Calvin. Calvin's doctrine of predestination was closely linked to his vision of God as absolutely powerful and perfect and humankind as completely powerless and corrupt. According to Calvin, from before they were even born, some people were predestined by God to spend eternity in heaven and others in hell. Because all humans were inherently sinful and God was, above all, a god of justice, the Almighty had doomed most men and women for eternal damnation and only a relative few for salvation and eternal life. Calvin emphasized that nothing a person did during his or her time on earth had any effect whatsoever on their predetermined status as saved or damned. Good works could not secure God's saving grace: nor could prayer, church attendance, or other expressions of piety.

Taking Calvin's doctrine of predestination as their starting point, English Puritans developed several other important theological concepts during the late sixteenth and early seventeenth centuries. Two of the most influential of these, the covenant of works and the covenant of grace, centered on how and why God came to give the gift of salvation to the "Elect," as the Puritans called the fortunate few who had been predestined to spend eternity in heaven. According to Puritan theology, the relationship between God and mankind was best understood in terms of covenants or contracts. After creating the world and the first man and woman, Adam and Eve, God established his first covenant with humanity, the covenant of works. Adam and Eve's responsibility within the covenant was to follow God's moral laws and obey Him in everything. For fulfilling their part of the contract, Adam and Eve, along with all their descendants, would be rewarded with everlasting life and perfect happiness. Urged on by the devil, however, Adam and Eve defied God by eating fruit from the forbidden Tree of the Knowledge of Good and Evil in the Garden of Eden. Their disobedience had lasting consequences for humankind.

Because of their bad behavior, the covenant of works was not only irrevocably broken, but all their descendents were also corrupted by this "original sin" in the Garden of Eden. Henceforth, every human being would come into the world with a natural bias toward evil and selfishness. They would be incapable of fully obeying God or understanding the true depth of their "depravity" (moral corruption).

Yet the God of Puritan theology was merciful as well as just. Therefore, although all people deserved to suffer eternal damnation on account of their sinful natures, God decided to give his human creations one more chance at redemption and eternal life. He allowed His son, Jesus Christ, to die on the cross in atonement for humankind's failings, so that some men and women might be saved from the fires of hell. As part of this new contract with humanity, known as the covenant of grace, God pledged to send his Holy Spirit to those whom he had predestined for salvation because of Jesus' sacrifice. When the Holy Spirit touched their souls or "converted" them, the Elect would finally be able to overcome their depraved natures. For the first time in their earthly lives, they would have the ability to truly comprehend and repent of their sins, have faith in Jesus Christ as their Savior, and become eligible for everlasting life.

A THEOLOGICAL DILEMMA

According to Calvin, no Christian could know for certain whether God had predestined his or her soul for conversion and salvation or for damnation. This created a major conceptual dilemma for Puritan ministers and theologians. If people's spiritual fates were decided before they were born, then what incentive did they have to obey the biblical commandments or society's laws or attend church every Sunday? No matter how well or how badly they behaved on

John Calvin founded the theory of predestination—the belief that no matter what a person does in his or her lifetime, he or she has already been predestined for heaven or hell. His writings and teachings formed the basis of Calvinism, a theological system that strongly influenced Puritanism.

earth, the Elect would receive God's grace and the damned would not. A hardened criminal could end up in heaven and a law-abiding, churchgoing citizen in hell. Clearly, a strict interpretation of the doctrine of predestination could lead to social and moral anarchy. Over time, Puritan divines devised two theological solutions to this sticky problem: sanctification and preparation.

Sanctification, the first idea developed by Puritan ministers to help persuade their flocks to follow God's moral laws, was designed to appeal to anxious parishioners who believed that they may have had a conversion experience but were unsure of its authenticity. To help answer their painful doubts and, at the same time, encourage good behavior among their parishioners, Puritan ministers argued that God gave more than just saving grace to His Elect. Once they had been converted, God also granted them the ability to lead morally upright and pious lives during the rest of their days on earth. Thus, while good deeds or regular church attendance could not win them a place among the Elect, people could interpret their pious thoughts and good behavior as a reassuring indication that they had received God's grace and had a secure spot in heaven. "Sanctification" is what the Puritans called an individual's new capacity for moral behavior after the Holy Spirit had touched their souls with saving grace. When a person had been sanctified, their ability to follow God's commandments would be apparent not only to themselves, but also to their fellow Puritans, who could recognize them as "visible saints," or members of the Elect.

A second concept that Puritan divines developed over the years to inspire believers to lead moral and pious lives was the doctrine of preparation. According to the concept, all Christians had a solemn obligation to prepare themselves for the possibility of receiving God's saving grace. Puritan ministers taught that preparing oneself for conversion involved rigorous study of the Bible, the only true source of standards for Christian belief and behavior, as well as an unflinchingly honest self-examination of one's spiritual and moral health. Such self-analysis would make the soul more humble and yielding and thus more receptive to receiving God's grace, the divines preached.

JOHN COTTON ON SALVATION

Anne Hutchinson's favorite minister, John Cotton, while careful not to publicly criticize his fellow Puritan clerics, took a different approach to the pressing questions of how salvation took place and how the Elect could know that they had been saved. In contrast to most Puritan divines of his day, Cotton did not regularly admonish his congregation to prepare themselves for the possibility of salvation or to scrutinize their behavior for signs that they had already been saved and sanctified. Rather, in his sermons at St. Botolph's, he emphasized God's boundless mercy in offering his gift of free grace to his unworthy creations and downplayed human effort in all aspects of conversion.

Cotton never said that scrutinizing one's outward behavior and inner moral health for evidence of salvation was wrong. In preaching and writing about God's saving grace, however, he emphasized a different pathway by which believers could determine whether they had been saved and were part of God's elect. This alternate pathway was grounded in an understanding of conversion as a dramatic spiritual event rather than the ongoing process most Puritan ministers portrayed it as. At the moment that they first received God's saving grace, Cotton suggested, converts typically feel a powerful sense of the Holy Spirit's loving presence within themselves. This mystical and deeply emotional experience would provide Christians with far greater confidence in their salvation than they could ever have from examining their outward behaviors or innermost thoughts for signs of sanctification. By 1630, Cotton was also suggesting in his sermons that those Christians who thought their souls had been touched by the Holy Spirit but still had doubts regarding the authenticity of their conversion might gain assurance of their Elect status by how they responded to particular biblical passages. Historian Michael Winship explains Cotton's method:

> There are scripture verses that, to Puritans, made direct, absolute promises of salvation: Isaiah 43:25, for example, "For mine own sake will I put away thy transgressions [sins]," or I Timothy 1:15. "Jesus Christ came into the world to save sinners, of which I am chief." You might have heard and mulled over such a verse many times. But at some point, according to Cotton, if you were among the saved, you would experience it as having a new, compelling power, as if it were speaking to you directly. That power came from its now being in fact a personal message from God carried by the Holy Spirit. . . . Words in the verse like "thy transgressions" or "I am chief" now referred to you personally, and God was thereby revealing to you that He had saved you. Because of the darkness of the human mind, you might not notice these revelations at first. But Cotton promised they would continue and eventually bring us to unspeakable joy.

A FAMILY TRAGEDY AND A SPIRITUAL CRISIS

From statements she made later in Massachusetts Bay, it is evident that Anne Hutchinson was immediately drawn to John Cotton's distinctive views regarding how conversion occurs and how an individual can know whether he or she has truly been saved. She was particularly attracted to Cotton's emphasis on conversion as a highly mystical and emotional event, rather than a primarily intellectual process for which Christians could prepare through scriptural study, good deeds, and pious thoughts.

At some point, probably in the late 1620s or in early 1630, Anne underwent a dramatic conversion experience of her own in which she felt the loving presence of the Holy Spirit, just as Cotton had described in his sermons and writings. Yet the mystical bliss and deep assurance of God's love Hutchinson felt at the moment of her conversion did not last. Anne descended into a painful spiritual crisis as she became racked with doubts regarding whether her soul had really been touched by God's saving grace. Perhaps, she worried, she had been deluded by the devil into imagining she was among the Elect. Desperate to regain assurance of her salvation, she turned to the time-honored Puritan practice of scrutinizing her thoughts and actions for evidence that she had been sanctified. Yet, in the end, her efforts only left her more uncertain than ever regarding her spiritual health, and her despair deepened.

Anne never pinpointed the exact month or year that her crisis of faith occurred. Most of her biographers, however, believe that her spiritual crisis had its roots in a devastating double tragedy that struck the Hutchinson family in 1630. According to parish records, in early September 1630, Anne and William's second child and first-born daughter, Susanna, died at the age of 16. Then, scarcely a month later, their seventh child, 8-year-old Elizabeth, also died. In the wake of the girls' deaths, grief and shock overwhelmed Anne. By this time, she had already lost one other child, William, who was born in 1623. For some reason, the date of his death does not appear in the Alford parish records, but Anne's biographer Eve LaPlante believes that he died sometime between 1626 and 1629. According to a history of Alford, for nearly a year after Susanna and Elizabeth's deaths, Anne became a virtual recluse in her own home: "For twelve months Anne withdrew from her neighbors seeking solace [comfort] from her religious beliefs."

Although historians cannot say with certainty how Susanna and Elizabeth died, it is generally assumed that the two girls were victims

Many believe that Hutchinson's daughters Susanna and Elizabeth were victims of the Black Death, a version of the bubonic plague that devastated world populations in the mid-fourteenth century. Hutchinson's grief launched her into a spiritual crisis as she began to question her religious beliefs and her faith in God.

of the bubonic plague. One of the most feared diseases in human history, the plague, also known as the Black Death, swept through Europe during the mid-1300s, claiming an estimated 25 million to 45 million lives, or about 33 percent to 60 percent of Europe's population. Although Europe never again experienced a plague pandemic on the magnitude of the one that occurred in the fourteenth century, parts of Europe, including England, continued to suffer regular outbreaks of the disease until the early eighteenth century. The bubonic plague visited a number of market towns and cities in Lincolnshire County during the late 1620s, and in June 1630, the disease arrived in Alford, where it struck with a vengeance. By the time the illness had run its course eight months later, 140 people, out of an estimated total population of 700 to 800 had died. At the outbreak's height in late July and early August of 1630, one particularly hard-hit family lost six of its members, five of them children, in a space of just 12 days.

As the plague claimed more and more lives in Alford during the summer of 1630, the town's weekly market days were canceled and its population quarantined in an effort to keep the devastating

THE BUBONIC PLAGUE

The most common symptoms of the bubonic plague are fever, chills, extreme exhaustion, aching joints, headache, vomiting, and buboes, the egg-shaped lumps that gave the disease its name. Typically located in the groin, armpits, or neck, these painful swellings result from a build-up of plague-carrying germs and dead cells in the sufferer's lymph nodes. Most people become ill with the bubonic plague with six days of being infected by the *Yersinia pestis* bacillus. Until antibiotic drugs were developed in the mid-twentieth century, bubonic plague typically killed three out of five of those who contracted the disease, with death most often occurring four days after the onset of symptoms. Two less-common variants of the plague, septicemic plague, in which *Yersinia pestis* bacillus directly invades the bloodstream, and pneumonic plague, in which it invades the lungs, are even more lethal. If left untreated, these two close relations of the bubonic plague are nearly 100 percent fatal.

illness from spreading to nearby communities. Many stricken Alford families were forced to rely on neighboring villages for food. A tall rock with a shallow indentation on its top was placed at the summit of Miles Cross Hill, overlooking the town. Hungry townspeople who were healthy enough to climb the steep hill placed money that had been disinfected in vinegar in the indentation. After the townspeople descended the hill, farmers and merchants from outlying areas placed grain, vegetables, and other food at the base of the stone in exchange for the sanitized coins. In this way, they were able to avoid all physical contact with the people of Alford. Person-to-person contact does not actually spread bubonic plague, but Hutchinson's contemporaries had no way of knowing that. It was not until the late nineteenth century that scientists realized that people contract the disease from being bitten by a flea that has ingested the blood of a rodent, typically a rat, infected with *Yersinia pestis,* a rod-shaped bacterium (the singular form of the word bacteria).

ANNE HAS A REVELATION

After many long months of grieving for her dead children and despairing over the state of her soul, Anne's spiritual crisis finally came to an end, probably sometime in the autumn or early winter of 1631. Six years later, during her trial in Massachusetts Bay for slandering the colony's ministers, she explained to the General Court, the colony's highest legislative and judiciary body, how she finally overcame her agonizing crisis of faith back in England. The turning point came when she decided to follow John Cotton's advice to believers who doubted the authenticity of their conversions and look to the Holy Scriptures for assurance. If a person was truly among the Elect, she remembered Cotton preaching, then one day when he was reading a biblical passage about God's gift of saving grace to sinners, he would suddenly have an overwhelming conviction that the verses were more than merely words on a page. No matter how many times he had studied the biblical passage before, he would now understand it in an entirely new light as a direct, personal message from the Holy Spirit to his soul.

To open her mind and heart as totally as possible to the message of spiritual reassurance that she hoped awaited her, Anne withdrew from her family and locked herself away in the quiet of her bedchamber for an entire day. As she leafed through her Bible, picking out passages on God's gift of grace, she had a strong sensation of the Holy Spirit's presence, just as Cotton had promised would happen to the Elect. The Holy Spirit revealed to her the "atheism" that had been lurking in her heart when she had tried to discover evidence of her salvation in her good deeds and thoughts rather than in Christ. At last assured of the genuineness of her conversion experience, Anne prayed to the Holy Spirit to deepen her understanding of God's will through the medium of His Holy Word. Randomly opening her Bible, she found herself staring at Chapter 9, verse 16 of the Book of Hebrews in the Old Testament. (The Old Testament is what Christians call the first half of the Bible; it corresponds to the Hebrew Scriptures.) "For where a testament [will or covenant] is, there must also of necessity be the death of the testator"(a person who makes a will or covenant), the passage read. As Anne, with her extensive knowledge of the Bible and theology knew, Puritan divines interpreted the term "testator" in the verse to mean Jesus Christ. The term "testament" signified the covenant of grace, by which God agreed to offer his saving grace to some sinners in exchange for Jesus' sacrificial death on the cross.

As Anne repeated the verse to herself, she later told her examiners in the General Court, she heard God's voice within her, saying: "He that denies the testament, denies the testator." In other words, he who rejects the covenant of grace and clings to the old covenant of works, by which God had promised eternal life to Adam and his descendents in return for their good behavior, rejects Jesus Christ Himself. After more reflection and prayer, Anne concluded that God was trying to convey an urgent warning to her regarding the Christian clergy: Any minister who "did not teach the *new* covenant [the covenant of grace] had the spirit of antichrist." (According to the Book of Revelation in the New Testament, the second half of the Christian Bible, the antichrist is the archenemy of Jesus Christ.) If Anne had assumed that this spiritual revelation only applied to non-Puritan ministers—the Anglican and Roman Catholic clerics whom Puritan divines had traditionally accused of preaching a covenant of works linking salvation to good deeds—then the rest of her life might have followed a very different course. Hutchinson, however, was convinced that the preachers who were doing the devil's work by holding onto the old covenant of works included a majority of Puritan divines as well as Catholic and orthodox Anglican ministers in Lincolnshire. True, the Puritan clerics did not go so far as to say that Christians could earn God's saving grace through their virtuous actions and pious thoughts. Nonetheless, the ministers' emphasis on a believer's obligation to prepare for salvation and ability to follow God's moral laws as evidence of conversion might lead many in their flocks to that heretical conclusion, Anne thought. (A heretical belief is one that differs from traditional or established religious doctrine.) For now, she would keep to herself her views regarding the grave doctrinal errors of ministers who taught the traditional Puritan concepts of preparation and sanctification. Despite her silence, the seeds of the controversy that would eventually make Anne Hutchinson the most famous female leader in colonial America had been sown.

5

Abandoning England for America

By 1632, two years before she left her homeland for America, Anne Hutchinson had come to the conclusion that there were only two preachers in all of Lincolnshire County worth hearing. The first was her beloved spiritual guide, John Cotton. The second was John Wheelwright, a follower of Cotton's and the vicar of the small Anglican church in Bilsby, one mile (1.6 km) northeast of Alford. Historians cannot say when Anne first became acquainted with Wheelwright. By 1630, however, she must have known the Bilsby vicar well, since Wheelwright married her husband William's younger sister, Mary, that year.

Anne's admiration for Cotton and Wheelwright was based on the two Puritan ministers' teachings on human involvement in the salvation process, an issue that had weighed heavily on her ever since she suffered a crisis of faith about the authenticity of her own conversion. Unlike most of their colleagues in the Anglican Church—orthodox as well as Puritan—Cotton and Wheelwright downplayed the convert's efforts in the drama of salvation. The idea that a believer could actively prepare himself to receive God's saving grace and find assurance of his Elect status in his ability to live a sanctified (holy) life had become widely accepted among the Puritan clergy and laity (nonclergy) by the early 1600s. In the wake of her spiritual crisis regarding her own Elect status, however, Anne had come to see the doctrines of preparation and sanctification as dangerous departures from the covenant of grace, in which God promised his saving grace to undeserving sinners in return for Jesus' sacrifice on the cross. Because Cotton and Wheelwright minimized the role of human conduct before, during, and after conversion, focusing instead on God's free and completely unearned gift of grace, Anne became convinced that they alone were preaching the true Christian message as revealed in the Holy Scriptures.

Yet, to Hutchinson's dismay, by mid-1632 both Cotton and Wheelwright had been forced from their Lincolnshire pulpits as part of a repressive anti-Puritan campaign by the Church of England's top leadership. Anne was deeply disappointed when Wheelwright was barred from preaching early that year, supposedly for attempting to sell church offices to job seekers, but actually because of his outspoken Puritanism. Cotton's decision to abandon his Boston church that spring in response to escalating persecution by his Anglican superiors hit Hutchinson even harder. "Great as was her esteem for her brother-in-law," writes Emery Battis, "for Anne Hutchinson it was always Cotton's light which burned most brightly."

WILLIAM LAUD'S ANTI-PURITAN CRUSADE

For most of John Cotton's tenure at St. Botolph's Church, he had had remarkably few run-ins with the Anglican leadership, despite his obvious Puritan leanings. Early in Cotton's career at St. Botolph's, Bishop Monteigne of Lincoln did briefly silence him for refusing to insist that his congregation kneel at communion, a practice that Puritans scorned as popish. Fortunately for Cotton, however, in 1621, the diocese of Lincoln received a new bishop, a tolerant and scholarly churchman from Wales named John Williams. Despite his own orthodox religious views, Williams was refreshingly open-minded regarding the presence of Puritan clergy in the Anglican Church. In time, Bishop Williams even came to admire the erudite (scholarly) and unfailingly diplomatic vicar of his diocese's biggest church, St. Botolph's. In Williams's opinion, "unlike most Puritans," Cotton "did not appear to be a zealot but preached a more gentle species of Calvinism and pursued his nonconformity quietly." (In this quotation, "nonconformity" means the failure to conform to expected Anglican standards or values.) Indeed, Cotton was widely known for his conciliatory personality. One friend and fellow Puritan minister described him as enjoying "a sweet temper of Spirit, whereby he could placidly [peacefully] bear those that differed from him in their apprehension [views]."

Having won Bishop Williams's admiration and support, Cotton felt free to quietly ignore those Anglican practices and rites he considered as being too Catholic, such as kneeling at communion or making the sign of the cross over the infant during baptism. By the end of the 1620s, however, Cotton had begun to worry about his own future and that of his Puritan clerical colleagues within the Anglican Church. His concerns were directly linked to the growing national influence of one of the Puritans' fiercest critics since the religious movement first developed during Queen Elizabeth's reign, Bishop William Laud.

Laud's close relationship with King Charles I, who inherited the throne from his father, James I in 1625, was the chief reason for his expanding power during the late 1620s. An even firmer foe of

Puritanism than his father, Charles considered the virulently anti-Puritan Laud as his most trusted spiritual adviser. Shortly before his coronation, Charles reportedly ordered Laud, then the bishop of St. David's in Wales, to put together a list of every Anglican clergyman in his kingdom and mark each name with an "O" for orthodox or a "P" for Puritan. Over the next three years, Charles helped Laud obtain a succession of increasingly prestigious ecclesiastical and political positions. In 1628, Laud was promoted to the bishopric of London and a year later to the chancellorship of Oxford University. Around the same time, Charles also increased his favorite churchman's political clout by making him one of his privy councilors. The Privy Council was personally assembled by the monarch and was made up of his most valued political advisers.

Laud's influence expanded into the judicial realm during the late 1620s as well, with dire consequences for England's Puritan minority. As a privy councilor, Laud automatically became a member of the Star Chamber, a court of justice first organized in 1487 during the reign of Henry VII and controlled by the monarch. The Star Chamber's chief purpose was to try high-ranking clergymen and aristocrats too powerful to be prosecuted in England's ordinary common-law courts. Under Charles and his father, James I, the Star Chamber became increasingly autocratic in its practices. The tribunal's proceedings were conducted in strict secrecy, with no juries and no right of appeal, and its punishments were often severe. Although the judges of the Star Chamber could not impose the death penalty, they could order floggings, branding, mutilation, and other harsh corporal punishments as well as lengthy prison sentences. With Charles's enthusiastic backing, by the early 1630s Laud was using his positions in the feared Star Chamber and the Church's supreme ecclesiastical court, the Court of High Commission, to intimidate and harass England's Puritan minority and force uniform practices of worship on all Anglican parishes. Dozens of Puritan ministers were summoned before the

With the support of King Charles I, William Laud launched a crusade to persecute Puritans, forcing leaders like John Cotton to leave England.

two courts in London to faces charges of unorthodoxy. If convicted, the clerics faced heavy fines, exile, or imprisonment. Laud also began pressuring members of the Anglican leadership whom he suspected of protecting Puritan clergymen in their dioceses, including John

Cotton's champion, Bishop Williams, to either join in his Puritan witch hunt or face the possibility of legal prosecution themselves.

During most of 1631 and early 1632, as Laud's anti-Puritan crusade continued to pick up steam, Cotton was on an extended leave of absence from St. Botolph's because of ill health. Soon after Cotton finally returned to his pulpit in the spring of 1632, he received a summons from Bishop Laud to appear before the High Court of Commission to explain his unorthodox practices. Fearful of being sent to prison, and urged on by his supporters to "fly for your safety" rather than answer the summons, Cotton went into hiding, eventually ending up in the London home of fellow Puritan John Davenport. In September, Cotton wrote to his wife from his London hideaway, warning her not to join him there just yet: "If you should now travel this way, I fear you will be watched and dogged at the heels."

COTTON, WINTHROP, AND THE "CITY ON A HILL"

Cotton could not hide from Laud and the High Court of Commission indefinitely. By the spring of 1633, he had come to the painful conclusion that he had no choice but to flee England. Laud's appointment that summer as Archbishop of Canterbury, the most powerful position in the Church of England after the English monarch, only made Cotton more certain that he must abandon his homeland.

By the time Laud was consecrated as Archbishop of Canterbury, Cotton had decided to seek asylum from his Anglican persecutors 3,000 miles (4,800 km) away from England, in the infant colony of Massachusetts Bay. After Cotton went into hiding in the spring of 1632, he had received a letter from the colony's Puritan governor, John Winthrop, urging him to come to Massachusetts. Winthrop, a devout Puritan lawyer and landowner from Suffolk County, was greatly impressed by Cotton's reputation as an outstanding preacher and biblical scholar. Winthrop had first tried to talk Cotton into emigrating to Massachusetts Bay two years earlier, when he led a group of some 800 English Puritans across the Atlantic to found the colony in April 1630. Yet, although Cotton agreed to deliver the farewell sermon to Winthrop's group before they set sail for America, he firmly declined the governor's invitation to go with them. Before he was confronted with the very real possibility of being sent to prison for his unorthodoxy, Cotton never doubted that his God-given mission was to remain in England and try to purify the Anglican Church from within.

Though they had chosen to leave England, like John Cotton, Winthrop and the other Puritans who set off for Massachusetts Bay in April 1630 were deeply committed to reforming the Anglican Church according to their religious principles. As long as the oppressive Charles I and Laud held power, however, the emigrants had come to believe that it was pointless, not to mention downright dangerous, for Puritans to remain in England in hopes of remaking the Anglican Church from within. Therefore, in 1629 a group of Puritan merchants and investors formed the Massachusetts Bay Company, a joint-stock corporation, and obtained a royal charter authorizing them to found a new colony in New England. (In seventeenth-century England, a joint stock-company was a type of corporation in which members pooled their stock or shares and paid the crown for the right to establish trade and colonies in the New World.) The Massachusetts Bay Company's royal charter granted the corporation territory from just south of the Charles River, in what is today eastern Massachusetts, to just north of the Merrimack River in present-day New Hampshire.

As far as the royal government was aware, the Massachusetts Bay Colony was a trading company organized for commercial gain. In reality, its Puritan backers were motivated primarily by spiritual rather than economic goals. Above all, they wanted Massachusetts Bay to serve as a religious refuge, where Puritan believers could

THE PILGRIMS

The nearly 1,000 Puritans under the leadership of John Winthrop who arrived in Massachusetts Bay in the summer of 1630 were not the first Puritans to emigrate to New England. In the autumn of 1620, a group of "Separatist" Puritans—or the Pilgrims, as they came to be known—sailed to America on the *Mayflower* and founded New England's first permanent settlement, Plymouth Colony.

The vast majority of Puritans in seventeenth-century England were committed to reforming the Anglican Church's practices and teachings. The most radical wing of the Puritan movement, the Separatists, had no reservations about abandoning the Church of England, however. They thought that their country's established church had become so corrupt that it was beyond reform and wanted to found their own separate church. Because the Dutch government was considerably more tolerant of religious dissenters than England's rulers were, during the late sixteenth and early seventeenth centuries, some English Separatists fled to Holland.

practice their faith freely, far from the interference of their authoritarian king and his henchmen in the Church of England. The new colonial venture soon attracted the attention of other middle- and upper-class Puritans, including John Winthrop. A man of strong opinions and a natural leader, Winthrop was determined that the Massachusetts Bay Colony be as independent of royal and Anglican influence as possible. Consequently, when the stockholders of the Massachusetts Bay Company elected him as their leader, or governor, in late 1629, Winthrop refused to accept the position until they agreed to transfer the corporation's headquarters from London to New England. This bold move by the company meant that, for all

In 1608, the Separatist group to which the Pilgrims belonged migrated to Holland, eventually settling in the city of Leyden. After about 10 years there, however, some of the group had become disgruntled with life in Holland and voted to settle in Virginia, on land that was under the jurisdiction of a London-based joint stock company. About 40 Separatists, joined by another 60 non-Separatist English laborers, boarded the *Mayflower* in September 1620, bound for northern Virginia. After the ship was blown off course near the New England coast, however, the emigrants ended up by settling outside of the territories controlled by the joint-stock company at Plymouth, in present-day Massachusetts, about 40 miles (64 km) south of Boston.

After a particularly difficult first winter during which half of the new colonists died, Plymouth Colony began to grow, but at a far slower rate than its neighbor to the north from 1630 on, the Massachusetts Bay Colony. By the last decade of the seventeenth century, Plymouth had been totally absorbed into the considerably more populous and economically prosperous Bay Colony.

intents and purposes, Winthrop and his fellow settlers would be able to run their political and religious affairs as they saw fit.

In keeping with the emigrants' commitment to reforming their "dear Mother," as they called the Anglican Church, Winthrop envisioned the colony as a model of true Christian worship for English Protestants, and Christians everywhere, to imitate. In a famous sermon delivered aboard the *Arbella*, the Puritan fleet's flagship, Winthrop told his listeners that their New World community was to be like a shining city set high on a hill top, a beacon of spiritual light in a dark and corrupt world. In their New England refuge, Winthrop declared, "we shall be as a city on a hill, the eyes of all people are

Like John Cotton, John Winthrop (*above*) believed that the Anglican church could be reformed from within, but he did not think it could be done while King Charles I was in power. Offering safety and protection from England's anti-Puritan crusade, Winthrop asked Cotton to come to the Massachusetts Bay Colony in the New World.

upon us." Should the Puritan colonists prove unworthy of their "special commission" from God to create a model Christian society, he warned, "the Lord will surely break out in wrath against us . . . [and]

we shall surely perish out of the good land whither we pass over this vast sea to posses it."

John Cotton must have been comforted by Winthrop's vision of Massachusetts Bay as "a city on a hill" that would convert England by its example as he prepared to finally leave his beloved homeland and church in the summer of 1633. Sometime in early July—the exact date of his departure from England is unknown—Cotton and his wife, Sarah, with the assistance of the renowned preacher's loyal supporters in London, sneaked aboard the sailing ship the *Griffin* to begin the two-month journey across the Atlantic to Massachusetts Bay. Midway through the long voyage, Cotton became a father for the first time at age 48 when Sarah gave birth to a healthy son. Cotton was greatly heartened by this happy turn of events. Whatever doubts he had harbored regarding his decision to emigrate had now been laid to rest. The safe birth of his first child at sea, Cotton was convinced, was a sure sign that the Almighty approved of his new mission to help create a model Puritan community in the American wilderness.

THE HUTCHINSONS MAKE A LIFE-CHANGING DECISION

Historians do not know when Anne first learned of Cotton's decision to abandon England for the Massachusetts Bay Colony. She was almost certainly aware of his plans by the late spring of 1633, however, when Cotton finally got around to officially resigning from his post as vicar of St. Botolph's in a letter to the Bishop of Lincoln, John Williams.

Anne was crushed by reports of Cotton's impending departure. She feared that she would never find another minister in England who preached about God's free gift of saving grace with equal understanding. At the same time, she was shocked and disheartened by the intensifying persecution of Puritans at the hands of royal and

Anglican authorities that had spurred Cotton to flee Boston for London a year earlier, and were now compelling him to leave England altogether. Just as she had done during her crisis of faith regarding the authenticity of her conversion, she leafed through her Bible in hope of receiving comfort and guidance from the Holy Spirit. Years later at her trial before the Massachusetts General Court, she would recall that her eyes were quickly drawn to a verse from the Book of Isaiah. "And though the Lord give you the bread of adversity, and the water of affliction, yet shall not thy teachers be removed into a corner any more, but thine eyes shall see thy teachers," the passage read (Isaiah 30:20). To Anne the verse's meaning was clear: God was telling her to follow her spiritual teacher, John Cotton, to the New World. The Holy Spirit further revealed to Anne that, although she would face hardships and dangers in America, the Lord would protect her. "Though . . . . [you] should meet with affliction," God's voice reassured her, "yet I am the same God that delivered Daniel out of the lion's den, I will also deliver thee."

Once she had made up her mind to follow her idol to Massachusetts, Anne had no trouble persuading William to emigrate. At a time when women were expected to submit to their husband's authority in all matters—religious, financial, or legal—William clearly respected his wife's opinions and wishes and considered her a full partner in their marriage. Several years later, John Winthrop, who by this point had come to despise both Hutchinsons, described William in his diary as henpecked and meek—"a man of very mild temper [disposition] and weak parts, and wholly guided by his wife." Yet there is ample evidence that William had powerful religious incentives of his own for emigrating, and was by no means "wholly guided by his wife" in choosing to settle in New England. In *Divine Rebel: The Life of Anne Marbury Hutchinson,* author Selma Williams points out that significantly more members of William Hutchinson's family than of Anne's family ended up migrating to the Puritan colony. Three of William Hutchinson's brothers, two of his sisters, and his elderly widowed mother undertook the long and arduous journey to Winthrop's "city on a hill," during the mid- to late 1630s, while just two of Anne's siblings emigrated to the New World. The fact that so many of William Hutchinson's relatives were such zealous Puritans that they were willing to forsake their native country for their faith indicates that Hutchinson's own Puritan convictions also ran deep, Selma Williams argues. Rather than William being a "weak follower, carting all his children to New England only because of [Anne's] insistent nagging," as John Winthrop implied in his diary, "all indications point to a mutually agreed upon decision to migrate," she contends.

Selma Williams and most of Anne's other biographers believe that the Hutchinsons had originally hoped to sail to Massachusetts in the summer of 1633 on the same ship as John Cotton. During the late winter of 1633, however, Anne became pregnant with her fourteenth child at the age of 42. This forced the couple to postpone their travel plans until after the baby's birth. In their stead, Anne and William sent their eldest child, 21-year-old Edward Hutchinson, to travel with Cotton to the New World on the *Griffin* in July 1633. Presumably, Edward's purpose in going ahead of his parents was to help prepare the way for them and his younger siblings' arrival in the colony the following summer.

Anne and William's baby, a girl whom they named Susan in honor of their deceased oldest daughter, Susanna, arrived in mid-November. Shortly afterward, they began the long and complex process of preparing to move to another continent. William sold his textile business to Anne's brother, John Marbury, and the couple started to dismantle their household. Many of the treasured possessions they had accumulated during 22 years of marriage, including large pieces of furniture such as cabinets and four-poster beds, had to be sold or given away since the family could only bring along items that could be readily carried. Among the necessities that they would have taken with them were trunks of clothing, tools of all types, pots and pans, building materials for their new house that would be impossible to obtain in Massachusetts such as glass windowpanes, and bolts of fabrics for William to sell in America.

Sometime in late spring 1634, Anne and William departed Alford for London. They were accompanied by 10 of their surviving 11 children (the eldest of the 11, Edward, was already in Massachusetts); Anne's younger sister Katherine and her husband; William's two middle-aged, unmarried cousins, Frances and Anne Freiston; and an unknown number of servants. In London, the Hutchinsons awaited news of a firm departure date for the *Griffin,* the same ship on which Edward and Cotton had traveled to Massachusetts the year before. The ship would sail only after its captain had secured sufficient numbers of passengers and cargo to make the 2- to 2½-month voyage across the Atlantic profitable. Finally, in late July, the Hutchinsons received word that the *Griffin* was ready to set sail for the New World.

For two monotonous and uncomfortable months, the Hutchinsons were crammed into the flimsy, unsanitary wooden sailing ship with nearly 100 other Puritan emigrants and their belongings; a crew of some 50 sailors and officers; a herd of 100 cattle; and dozens of chickens, geese, and pigs. Finally, on September 18, 1634, the *Griffin* docked in Boston, Massachusetts Bay's largest town and chief port, and home to most of the young colony's leading political and religious figures, including John Winthrop and John Cotton. At last Anne could look forward to practicing her Christian faith freely under the wise guidance of her idol John Cotton and without interference from the king of England or his bishops. Little could she have imagined then how quickly she would become disillusioned with the Puritans' New World Promised Land.

6

Anne Becomes Controversial

After Anne and William Hutchinson arrived in Boston in September 1634, they immediately began to carve out a place for themselves in their new community. One of their first tasks was to apply for membership in the institution that was at the heart of their new hometown's religious and social life: its only church, the First Church of Boston. (Bostonians did not build a second meeting-house, as the Puritans called their churches, until 1650, after the town's population had doubled from about 700 in the mid-1630s to approximately 1,400.)

ANNE'S ROCKY START IN THE NEW WORLD

All residents of an Anglican parish were automatically members of their local church in England. In contrast, church membership in Puritan New England was looked upon as a privilege. Although everyone was required by law to attend weekly services at their town's Puritan meetinghouse, full church membership was restricted to those men and women who could provide convincing evidence to their ministers that they had received God's saving grace. Typically, both an applicant's personal testimony and good behavior were considered in determining whether he or she was among the Elect. During the mid-1630s, just under half of the Massachusetts Bay Colony's 5,000 inhabitants were church members.

William and Anne Hutchinson applied together for membership in the First Church in late October 1634. William progressed through the admission process rapidly and was admitted on October 26. Anne's experience was very different. Unlike William, she had to undergo extensive questioning by the church's two ministers, John Wilson and John Cotton, before finally being granted membership a full week after her husband. The reason for the ministers' extraordinary caution regarding Anne's application for membership was a complaint they had received about her from one of her fellow passengers on the *Griffin*, the Reverend Zechariah Symmes of Dunstable, England.

One hot August afternoon about a month into the *Griffin*'s transatlantic voyage, Symmes had preached a rambling, four-hour sermon to his shipmates on the subject of sanctification. In his sermon, Symmes argued that an individual's unselfish behavior toward others provided powerful evidence that he or she had been saved. As Anne sat in the blazing summer sun listening to the long-winded preacher, she became increasingly irritated by what she viewed as Symmes's unbiblical emphasis on good works in the salvation process. During the discussion period following the sermon, she finally erupted, accusing Symmes of teaching the old, discredited covenant of works when he should have been teaching the covenant of grace. Symmes was incensed that a layperson, much less a female layperson, would be so impudent as to cast doubt on his doctrinal purity. As soon as the *Griffin* arrived in Boston, he rushed off to inform the Reverends Wilson and Cotton of Anne's disrespectful behavior. Symmes urged the ministers to scrutinize Hutchinson's theological opinions, which he suspected of being "corrupt," as well as her general moral character, before inviting the impertinent housewife to join their church.

At Symmes's insistence, Wilson and Cotton subjected Anne to an unusually long and searching religious examination after she and William formally applied for membership in the First Church. Symmes, however, must have been disappointed by the outcome of Anne's interrogation. She "gave full satisfaction" of her doctrinal soundness in all of her answers, Cotton and Wilson reported. Whatever differences there might be in her theological views and their own were insignificant, the two divines declared, and posed no barrier to her admittance to the church. Accordingly, on November 2, 1634, Anne Hutchinson joined her husband as a full member of the First Church of Boston. Later, after he had soured on Anne, John Winthrop said that she "cunningly dissembled [disguised] and colored" her true religious opinions in order to worm her way into the First Church. At the time, however, neither he nor any other member of Boston's political or religious elite voiced the slightest concern about Anne's religious or moral character, despite Symmes's warnings about her insolent attitude and "corrupt" theological beliefs. Indeed, within a few months of coming to Massachusetts, both Anne and William had not only firmly established themselves within the top rungs of Boston society, but were also well on their way to becoming respected community leaders.

SETTLING IN

Despite the embarrassing delay in Anne's admission to the First Church, the Hutchinsons received a warm welcome from the

The Hutchinsons arrived in Boston in September 1634 and began adjusting to life in Massachusetts. Their colony was built around the church, and all community members were required to attend weekly sermons. Only a minority of churchgoers were granted full membership in New England's Puritan churches, however.

Boston community. Bostonians were deeply impressed both by William's wealth—he reportedly brought the substantial sum of "one thousand guineas in gold" with him to America—and Anne's high social rank as a member of Lincolnshire's landed gentry. Puritans did not believe in social and economic equality. Instead, they assumed that it was part of God's plan for the world that some people would always be wealthier and more influential than others. As John Winthrop explained it, "God Almighty in His most holy and wise providence hath so disposed of the condition of mankind as in all times some must be rich, some poor; some high and eminent in power and dignity; others mean [poor] and in subjection." Accordingly, during the Bay Colony's early years, the amount and location of the land that town officials granted to a head of a household was almost always decided by his financial and social standing back in England. The Puritans' inequitable system of land distribution definitely worked in William and Anne's favor. "At a time when social and geographic place mattered deeply, the Hutchinsons were assigned a house lot directly across from Governor Winthrop, and William was allotted six hundred acres, a clear acknowledgement of his rank, since he was a merchant, not a farmer," notes historian Marilyn Westerkamp. In addition to his desirably located house lot and 600-acre (242.8 hectares) farm just south of Boston in Wollaston (later called Quincy), Hutchinson in July 1635 was granted his own private island in Boston Harbor, which he used for grazing his large flock of sheep.

Across the lane from John Winthrop and his wife, Margaret, and just a short walk from the First Church, the Hutchinsons built one of the biggest houses in Boston. When the Hutchinsons first arrived in Massachusetts Bay, most Bostonians still lived in simple, one-room cottages, even though the average Puritan household consisted of 9 to 10 people—two adults and 7 or 8 children. The Hutchinsons, however—like their prominent neighbors, the Winthrops—had the financial resources to construct a spacious and comfortable two-story house complete with six rooms, including a downstairs parlor (living room). Directly next to his new house, William built a wooden shelter to store and display the fine cloth he had brought with him from Alford, and his transplanted textile business soon thrived. Before long he had carved out an important niche for himself not only in his adopted home's economic life, but in its political life as well. In May 1635, Hutchinson was elected as a deputy to the Massachusetts General Court. Soon after, he was also chosen as one of Boston's selectmen (a member of a board of officials who administered the towns of the Massachusetts Bay Colony).

While her husband was making his mark in Boston's political and economic affairs, Anne was establishing herself as one of the town's most valuable and popular female citizens. Just as she had back in Alford, Anne gave generously of her time to her neighbors as a midwife and folk healer, devoting countless hours to assisting them at childbirth and in illness. Her compassion for those in need, combined with her many years of experience in delivering babies and preparing herbal remedies, quickly won her the trust and gratitude of the Boston community. "Being a woman very helpful in times of childbirth and other occasions of bodily infirmities, and well furnished for means of those purposes, she easily insinuated herself into the affections of many," John Winthrop later wrote about Anne's rapid rise to prominence in her adopted hometown of Boston.

ANNE'S EXPANDING RELIGIOUS ROLE

When she was supervising at births, which were heavily attended by the expectant mother's female neighbors and relatives just as they had been in England, or tending to the ill, Anne took every opportunity to share her spiritual beliefs and wisdom with her patients and their families and friends. "Her ordinary talk was about the things of the Kingdom of God," recalled Winthrop, and Anne quickly became known throughout Boston for her deep knowledge of the Holy Scriptures as well as her piety.

By the summer of 1635, Hutchinson had begun holding regular religious meetings in her home for her continually expanding circle of female acquaintances in Boston. The private get-togethers were similar to those she had led in her Alford parlor, except that instead of clarifying difficult biblical passages for her listeners, Anne restated and explained the main themes of John Cotton's twice weekly sermons to them. Within days of Anne's admission to the church in early November, the Reverend Wilson had set sail for England to take care of pressing family business, leaving Cotton in full charge of the First Church. This turn of events suited Anne perfectly, since there was no other preacher she would rather listen to than her beloved spiritual guide, John Cotton. Most of the First Church's congregation also seemed quite content with the new arrangement. Immediately after Cotton's arrival in Boston in September 1633, they had invited him to share ministerial duties with Wilson, who had been the church's pastor ever since Winthrop and the first group of Puritan settlers founded Boston in 1630. Cotton's eloquent and emotionally powerful preaching had been an immediate hit with Bostonians. Indeed, during his first few months at the First Church, the charismatic Lincolnshire preacher sparked a major religious revival, resulting in an increase in church membership of more than 50 percent by the winter of 1634.

As time went on, Anne began to venture beyond merely summarizing the central points of Cotton's popular Sunday and Thursday sermons to his First Church flock by offering her own commentary on his lectures. Not surprisingly, the aspect of Cotton's preaching Anne most admired—his emphasis on God's free and unearned gift of grace—was what she chose to focus on at her religious meetings. She particularly emphasized Cotton's teachings regarding the potential pitfalls of the Puritan doctrine of sanctification. Cotton never went so far as to say that the doctrine of sanctification was false. He did, however, caution his listeners against placing too much weight on their good behavior as proof that their souls had been touched or "sealed" by the Holy Spirit. Zeroing in on this theme, Hutchinson repeatedly warned her listeners about the danger of assuming you had been saved based on your behavior rather than a sense of personal communion with the Holy Spirit, such as she herself had experienced. Hutchinson "would explain to the women just how easily they could fool themselves that they were in the covenant of grace while they were still in the covenant of works," writes historian Michael Winship: "They might engage in all the practices expected of godly laity: 'Prayer, Family Exercises, Conscience of Sabbaths, Reverence of Ministers, Frequenting of Sermons . . .,' and yet, Hutchinson ominously and terrifyingly warned them, they had never been truly, savingly converted."

John Winthrop would later accuse Anne of being a fear monger who deliberately spread a "false terror" among the devout women of Boston with her dire warnings about the close relationship between the doctrine of sanctification and the discredited covenant of works. "False" or not, the fear that she incited in the hearts and minds of her listeners regarding the true health of their souls proved remarkably effective. As John Cotton later recalled, many women who attended Anne's weekly meetings "were convinced, that they had gone on in a covenant of works, and were much shaken and humbled thereby, and brought to inquire more seriously after the Lord Jesus Christ." The results, at least in the beginning, were overwhelmingly positive, Cotton maintained. Hutchinson, he declared, "wrought [accomplished] with God, and with the Ministers, the work of the Lord . . . [and] found loving and dear respect from both our Church-Elders and Brethren, and so from my self."

THE GROWING POPULARITY OF ANNE'S MEETINGS

By the summer and early autumn of 1636, Hutchinson's private religious get-togethers had undergone several important changes. Firstly, they had become so popular that Anne decided to hold two meetings in her home every week, instead of just one. Secondly,

Because she was a woman, Hutchinson could not be ordained as a min-ister in the Puritan church. Nonetheless she conducted weekly meetings in her Boston home and soon gained a loyal following, which threatened religious leaders.

men, including some of the Boston community's most prominent members, had begun attending her sessions. Lastly, Anne's comments on her favorite topic—the covenant of grace—had taken on an increasingly militant and divisive tone as she began to question the doctrinal soundness of Cotton's colleague at the First Church, John Wilson.

By mid-1636, as many as 80 people, male as well as female, were crowding into Anne's parlor every week for her religious meetings, drawn not only by her impressive mastery of theology and the Bible, but also by her striking self-confidence and air of spiritual authority. Among her new disciples were men of considerable status and influence, including several deputies to the General Court and three of the city's most successful businessmen and merchants: William Aspinwall, John Coggeshall, and William Coddington, the richest man in Boston. Far and away the most prominent of Anne's male followers, however, was Massachusetts Bay's new governor, Henry Vane. Vane, a zealous Puritan convert, was wealthy, aristocratic, and very well connected politically—his father was one of King Charles's closest advisers. Although he had just turned 23 and had only been in Massachusetts for seven months, Vane had been elected to serve as the colony's governor in its annual May elections, beating out John Winthrop and other more experienced candidates for the position.

At the same time that the size and makeup of Anne's audience was changing, the tone of her biweekly religious meetings was also undergoing an important transformation. The chief reason for this change was the return of the Reverend John Wilson to the First Church in late 1635 following a yearlong absence. Wilson had departed Massachusetts for England to attend to family business immediately after Anne was accepted into the First Church in November 1634. Consequently, she had had little, if any, opportunity to hear him preach. After Wilson rejoined Cotton in the pulpit in October 1635, Hutchinson received an unpleasant surprise. Over the next several months,

CHURCH AND STATE IN PURITAN NEW ENGLAND

In Massachusetts Bay, as was true throughout the rest of Puritan New England during the seventeenth century, although the colony was not officially a theocracy, in practice church and state were closely intertwined. (A theocracy is a state governed by or subject to religious authority.) For example, only church members—or more specifically, *male* church members—were allowed to vote in colony-wide and local political elections. Additionally, the government taxed all households to pay for ministers' salaries and the construction of new meetinghouses. To ensure the success of the godly society John Winthrop envisioned in his famous "city on a hill" sermon, he and Massachusetts' other founding fathers insisted that the state uphold and protect the one "true" faith and church—their own. Consequently, Massachusetts' civil officials were expected to suppress and punish anyone who expressed contempt for the colony's Puritan clergy, refused to attend weekly church services (or fell asleep during them), committed blasphemy (speaking irreverently of God), or held heretical opinions.

it became obvious to her that, in common with most of the Puritan ministers she had known back in England, Wilson was a firm supporter of the doctrines of preparation and sanctification. Wilson claimed to preach the covenant of grace. Anne, however, worried that by emphasizing good behavior as a means of preparing for divine grace and as evidence that a believer was already saved, he was really promoting a covenant of works among his flock.

During the spring and summer of 1636, Hutchinson became more and more upset whenever it was Wilson's turn to preach. Expressing contempt for a minister or his preaching was a crime in Puritan New England. Nonetheless, by mid-1636 she had begun to openly criticize Wilson at her private religious meetings, even going so far as to imply that his emphasis on human action in the conversion process meant that he had probably never been saved himself. Although there is no reason to believe that John Cotton knew what Anne was saying about his First Church colleague behind his back, one minister who was definitely aware of her increasingly harsh verbal attacks on Wilson was Anne's brother-in-law and friend, John Wheelwright. John and Mary Wheelwright had moved into the Hutchinsons' Boston home in May after immigrating to the Bay Colony from England, where Wheelwright had spent most of the previous three years hiding from the Anglican authorities after being forced out of his Bilsby pulpit. Aside from Cotton, Wheelwright had been the one minister in all of Lincolnshire County whose teachings on salvation Anne approved of.

CONTROVERSY ERUPTS IN THE FIRST CHURCH

Anne's close ties to Wheelwright and her outspoken admiration for his preaching endeared him to her followers in Boston, and in October, with Hutchinson's blessing, they decided to invite Wheelwright to serve as the First Church's third minister. Having Wheelwright share pulpit duties with Wilson and Cotton would provide them with more opportunities to hear the sort of preaching they liked, the Hutchinsonians reasoned, while at the same time lessening what they considered as Wilson's harmful spiritual influence over the First Church. (The term "Hutchinsonians" is often used by historians to refer to Anne's followers.)

When Wilson got wind of the Hutchinsonians' plan to recruit Wheelwright as his second ministerial colleague, he was deeply offended, viewing the effort as an attempt to undercut his authority in the church he had helped to found and had served loyally for almost six years. Resolved to block Wheelwright's appointment, Wilson turned for assistance to his longtime friend and the church's most prominent lay member after Governor Vane, John Winthrop. Winthrop, who had recently begun to hear disturbing rumors about the Hutchinsonians' unorthodox religious opinions and growing strength, rushed to Wilson's defense. At first it appeared that there was little he could do to prevent Wheelwright's appointment since the Hutchinsonians had become so numerous that they now made up a majority of the First Church's 150 members. Winthrop, however, was both resourceful and determined. By October 30, the date the church had chosen to vote on whether to hire Wheelwright, he had hit on a way to thwart the Hutchinsonians' plot to push Wilson into the background. Invoking a long-forgotten rule that required all decisions of the First Church's membership to be unanimous, Winthrop was able to stop the Hutchinsonians in their tracks at the meeting. Soon after, Wheelwright accepted an offer from a small Puritan church 10 miles away from Boston, in Mount Wollaston, to Winthrop's great relief. Yet, as Winthrop would soon discover, despite Wheelwright's departure from Boston, the divisive power struggle between Anne Hutchinson and her disciples and John Wilson and his supporters was far from over. Indeed, over the next few months the controversy would spread beyond the First Church to threaten the unity and peace of the entire Bay Colony.

7

Putting a Stop to the Rebellion

The failure of their scheme to lessen John Wilson's influence over the First Church by hiring John Wheelwright as a third minister did not discourage the Hutchinsonians. On the contrary, Anne and her disciples became even more open in their opposition to Wilson and his teachings on human effort in the salvation process. On at least one occasion, Anne rose from her pew and led a large group of her female disciples out of the meetinghouse while Wilson was preaching. Some of her followers also started harassing Wilson during the discussion periods following his sermons. According to Reverend Thomas Weld of the nearby First Church of Roxbury, during the question-and-answer sessions the Hutchinsonians accused Wilson of being everything from a "legalist," who cared more for moral laws than saving grace, to an "Opposer of Christ Himself." John Winthrop was appalled to witness his fellow church members, some of whom had known Wilson for many years and "witnessed what good he had done for the church . . . fall upon him with such bitterness."

At the same time that they were becoming more vehement and public in their attacks on Wilson, Anne and her disciples at the First Church were also taking their crusade against the doctrines of preparation and sanctification beyond their hometown. Members of Hutchinson's group began fanning out into the Massachusetts countryside on Sundays to evaluate the preaching of other ministers in the colony on human actions in the salvation process. They quickly concluded that all the clergymen, except John Wheelwright, shared Wilson's views on the issue. To the dismay of the ministers whose churches they visited, Anne's followers used the discussion periods following the sermon to blast the preacher's "defective" understanding of the conversion process in front of their entire congregation. Ever since Christ's crucifixion, humankind had lived under the covenant of grace, the Hutchinsonians would point out. Yet, they maintained, clergymen who preached the doctrines of preparation and sanctification were actually endorsing the covenant of works, in which people earned their way to heaven by their good behavior.

ANNE MEETS WITH THE MINISTERS

Late in the autumn of 1636, a group of 10 prominent ministers from towns throughout Massachusetts Bay gathered at John Cotton's house to try to get to the bottom of the widening theological controversy. Although Anne was only a layperson, and a female one at that, the clergymen urged Hutchinson to attend their meeting. By inviting Anne to "what was essentially a clerical conference," the ministers were clearly "acknowledging her leadership," contends Marilyn Westerkamp. "While they certainly denied her any legitimate claim to such a role," Westerkamp writes, "their actions unconsciously confirmed the strength of her spiritual authority."

During the conference, the ministers grilled Hutchinson on her theological beliefs, which some of her critics, including John Winthrop, had started to link to the so-called Antinomian heresy. Antinomianism, which means "against the law," was the belief that those chosen by God for salvation were free from having to follow His biblical commandments. Instead, the Elect could listen to the voice of God within themselves for moral as well as spiritual guidance. The religious and political leaders of Massachusetts Bay considered Antinomianism a particularly dangerous heresy. If each individual could communicate directly with God, as the Antinomians argued, then people would have little incentive to follow the laws of either church or state, the colony's orthodox leadership worried. Ministers and magistrates would lose all authority, public order would disintegrate, and the Puritan founders' dream of Massachusetts as a shining "city on a hill," a model of righteous Christian living for the rest of the world to follow, would be shattered.

Exactly what Anne said during the meeting at Cotton's house is a matter of dispute. What is certain is that the ministers' encounter with Hutchinson in the fall of 1636 was confrontational. Hutchinson denied being an Antinomian. In direct opposition to mainstream Puritan teaching on sanctification, however, she insisted that an inward sense of communion with the Holy Spirit was the *only* valid evidence that a person was among the Elect. Any cleric who taught his flock that godly behavior or outward piety could be taken as proof of salvation was guilty of preaching the covenant of works, she hotly accused, and was "not an able minister of the gospel." Hutchinson "was a woman not only difficult in her opinions, but also of an intemperate [unreasonable and unrestrained] spirit," Salem minister Hugh Peter had concluded by the end of the interview. Clearly, persuading Anne to accept their theological arguments and spiritual authority was going to be no easy task for Massachusetts' orthodox clergy. Since Anne and her disciples publicly referred to Cotton as their spiritual mentor, after questioning Hutchinson, Peter and the other ministers attending the meeting also interrogated Cotton regarding his views on salvation and on Hutchinson herself. Gentle and conciliatory by nature, Cotton was sympathetic toward Anne and urged that she and her supporters be treated with respect and tolerance. In direct contrast to Hutchinson's stated beliefs, however, he emphasized that both a direct experience with the Holy Spirit and sanctification could be taken as reliable evidence that a person had received God's saving grace. This satisfied the majority of Cotton's questioners, who concluded that the popular Boston preacher should not be held responsible for Anne's or her followers' unorthodox religious opinions or "insolent" behavior.

THE WHEELWRIGHT CONTROVERSY

As of late 1636, Anne counted among her followers most of the members of the First Church; a number of prominent Boston businessmen, including the town's wealthiest citizen; and, most importantly, Governor Henry Vane. Consequently, despite hers and her followers' bold attacks on the Massachusetts clergy and mainstream Puritan theology, the Hutchinsonians' orthodox opponents were hesitant to come down too hard on them. Still, the orthodox leadership agreed that something had to be done, and soon, to restore peace and harmony to the increasingly divided colony. Therefore, at their December meeting, the members of the General Court resolved to call a colony-wide Fast Day on January 19, 1637, so that the people of Massachusetts could pray together for God's forgiveness and healing for their strife-ridden community. Puritan authorities typically called general Fast Days after some natural calamity, such as a disease epidemic, flooding, or a bad harvest, had struck their community. On

Fast Days everyone was expected to refrain from eating or drinking and spend the entire day at their local meetinghouse, repenting of their sins and praying for God's mercy.

In a spirit of reconciliation, Cotton and Wilson invited John Wheelwright, the one Massachusetts minister closely associated with Hutchinson and her group, to speak at the First Church's Fast Day service in January 1637. As Wheelwright well knew, the people of Massachusetts had been ordered by the General Court to come together to pray for an end to the religious disagreements that had created so much bad feeling amongst them. Yet, rather than lecture on the need for understanding and unity, Wheelwright seemed determined to use his Fast Day sermon to fan the flames of dissension in the colony. Wheelwright began his lecture by blaming Massachusetts' current troubles squarely on "antichristian" ministers who insisted on preaching a covenant of works. To overcome the ministers' harmful influence, all true believers "must prepare for a spiritual combat, . . . put on the armor of God," and "show themselves valiant. They should have their swords ready, they must fight and fight with spiritual weapons," he declared. If Massachusetts was to survive as a godly community, Wheelwright cautioned, true believers had a sacred duty to stop their powerful "antichristian" opponents—"the greatest enemies to the state that can be"—from teaching false doctrine. Should that prove impossible, then the erring ministers, and the government officials who supported them, must be removed from positions of authority in the Bay Colony.

Not surprisingly, Wheelwright's belligerent sermon caused an uproar among the orthodox religious and political leaders of Massachusetts Bay. At the next meeting of the General Court in March 1637, a majority of its members found Wheelwright guilty of sedition for seeking to stir up the people against their leaders. (Sedition is behavior or language inciting rebellion against lawful authority.) The Court's harsh ruling against Wheelwright outraged

Hoping to settle the religious differences among colony members, church leaders invited John Wheelwright, Hutchinson's brother-in-law and friend, to speak to the community in a gesture of reconciliation. Wheelwright instead used the opportunity to publicly decry the ministers and political leaders of the Massachusetts Bay Colony.

the Hutchinsonians. Vane formally protested the ruling, and a majority of the First Church's male members submitted a strongly worded petition to the Court defending Wheelwright and demanding that the Court rescind its judgment. Throwing caution to the wind, the petition's authors daringly urged the Court to reflect on the possibility that Satan, "the ancient enemy of Free Grace," was actually behind their "persecution" of Wheelwright, noting that the Devil often "raised up such calumnies [slanders] against the faithful Prophets of God." Since women had no political rights in Massachusetts Bay, as was true in England and throughout most of the world at the time, the First Church's female members were not allowed to sign the petition to the General Court. Consequently, Anne Hutchinson's signature was not among the 58 that appeared on the appeal. Nonetheless, nearly all the men who did sign the document were known to be Anne's followers, leading Winthrop and others in the orthodox camp to conclude that Hutchinson was the true mastermind behind the defiant petition.

THE ORTHODOX GO ON THE OFFENSIVE

In hopes that the rebellious clergyman might yet repent and be brought back into the orthodox fold, the General Court voted to delay sentencing John Wheelwright until after the yearly general elections in May. At Winthrop's recommendation, the annual elections were moved from Boston, the political and spiritual center of the Hutchinsonian movement, to more conservative Cambridge, several miles away. Winthrop's Cambridge strategy proved successful. When the vote was counted, Winthrop, the favorite of the orthodox camp, had handily defeated the Hutchinsonians' loyal champion, Henry Vane, to reclaim Massachusetts' highest political office. About two months later, the humiliated ex-governor sailed back home to England.

With Vane, Anne's most influential supporter, gone, the tide turned decisively in favor of her orthodox opponents. Determined to stop the possible migration of additional Hutchinsonian recruits to the Bay Colony, the General Court passed a restrictive law declaring that newcomers could not purchase a house or remain in any Massachusetts town for more than three weeks without the government's explicit consent. The Court also ordered all the colony's ministers to attend a special synod, or assembly, to discuss the "dangerous" theological errors that had been circulating through Massachusetts Bay in recent months. The synod, which convened in Cambridge on August 30, eventually identified and condemned 82 doctrinal errors to be guarded against by Puritan New Englanders, most of them beliefs that had been attributed—fairly or unfairly—to Anne and her disciples. On September 22, the final day of the synod, the ministers passed a resolution banning large, female-led religious meetings of the type Anne had been holding in her Boston home, without actually mentioning Hutchinson by name. "That though women might meet (some few together) to pray and edify [educate] one another; yet such a set [fixed] assembly (as was then in practice at Boston), where sixty or more did meet every week, and one woman (in a prophetical way, by resolving questions of doctrine, and expounding Scripture) took upon her the whole exercise, is agreed to be disorderly, and without rule," the synod declared.

To the dismay of Winthrop and his orthodox allies, neither the General Court's conviction of Wheelwright in March for sedition nor the synod's resolution against large, female-led religious meetings six months later seemed to intimidate the Hutchinsonians in the least. Wheelwright stubbornly declined all opportunities to renounce his inflammatory sermon and Hutchinson went right on holding regular religious meetings in her parlor. Anne's disciples at the First Church also remained openly defiant. During the summer of 1637, some of her male followers even went so far as to refuse to serve in a Boston militia company assembled to fight the Pequot, a warlike Native

American tribe based in nearby Connecticut, because John Wilson was the company's chaplain.

With the Hutchinsonians now appearing to threaten the safety as well as the unity of Massachusetts Bay, Winthrop and the General Court's orthodox majority decided that the time had come to put a stop, once and for all, to the rebellious faction. Therefore, when the General Court reconvened for its autumn session in early November 1637 in Cambridge, its first priority was to finally punish the unrepentant Wheelwright for his "seditious" Fast Day sermon. On November 4, the Court, presided over by Governor Winthrop, voted to banish Wheelwright from Massachusetts, giving him two weeks to leave the colony. Accompanied by a small group of friends and supporters, Wheelwright headed northward out of Massachusetts, eventually founding the town of Exeter, New Hampshire.

Having dispensed with Wheelwright, the court next focused on the members of its own body who had backed Hutchinson and her brother-in-law throughout the escalating controversy: Boston deputies William Aspinwall, John Coggeshall, and John Oliver. All three Hutchinsonians were stripped of their duties as deputies to the court, and Coggeshall and Aspinwall were disenfranchised (deprived of their right to vote) as well. Aspinwall, who had reportedly helped compose the offensive petition to the General Court demanding that Wheelwright's conviction be overturned and implying that Satan had inspired his "persecution" by the orthodox camp, received the harshest punishment. He was banished from the Massachusetts Bay Colony for "seditious libel" against the authorities and for an "insolent . . . carriage [contemptuous manner]." Yet Aspinwall, Coggeshall, Oliver, and even Wheelwright were no more than the "branches" of the spiritual controversy that had threatened to tear apart his "city on a hill," Winthrop believed. The controversy's roots and trunk—Anne Hutchinson—still had to be dealt with. "The breeder and nourisher of all these distempers [disturbances]," as

Winthrop described Colonial America's first female religious leader, was to be brought to trial at last.

ANNE HUTCHINSON DEFENDS HERSELF

Anne Hutchinson's trial before the General Court began early on the morning of November 7, 1637, in the Cambridge meetinghouse, with John Winthrop presiding as chief prosecutor and judge. Winthrop launched the proceedings by briefly reviewing the prosecution's case. The government's chief charge against Hutchinson was sedition, the same crime for which Wheelwright had been brought to trial. Hutchinson had "troubled the peace of the commonwealth and the churches," and taken a "great share in the promoting and divulging [spreading] of those opinions" behind the recent religious divisions in Massachusetts, Winthrop declared. Moreover, he accused, she had encouraged and assisted the troublemakers whom the court had already "censured" for sedition; slandered the colony's ministers; and continued to lead large religious meetings in her house after the synod had prohibited such gatherings. Winthrop ended his speech by warning Hutchinson that should she refuse to acknowledge her errors and repent, then "the court may take such course that you may trouble us no further."

According to the laws of colonial Massachusetts, Anne did not have the right to hire a lawyer, meaning that she had to act as her own legal counsel throughout her trial. It was a task for which Hutchinson had been extraordinarily well prepared from early childhood on, when her chief textbook aside from the Bible was her father's account of his trial for slandering his superiors in the Anglican Church. Anne's unusual early education combined with her keen mind, courageous determination, and remarkable self-assurance allowed her to put Winthrop and her other orthodox prosecutors on the defensive time and time again during the course of what turned out to be nearly

With Wheelwright and other leading Hutchinson supporters either exiled or punished, the General Court commenced a trial against Hutchinson for sedition and slander. Hutchinson, who was pregnant with her fifteenth child, defended herself until it became clear that the court had predetermined her fate.

two full days of relentless questioning. Even Winthrop could not help but be impressed by Anne's resolve and self-confidence throughout her ordeal in Cambridge. He would later describe Hutchinson with a mixture of grudging admiration and scorn as "a woman of a haughty and fierce carriage, of a nimble wit [quick intellect] and active spirit, and a very voluable [smooth talking] tongue, more bold than a man" in argument.

Winthrop started his examination of Anne by sternly demanding whether she "did not justify [defend] Mr. Wheelwright's sermon and the petition." Instead of addressing his question, Hutchinson boldly turned the tables on the governor, demanding "What law have I broken?" After all, she pointed out, her signature was not even on the "seditious" petition blasting the magistrates for convicting Wheelwright and demanding that the ruling be overturned. Hutchinson had broken the Fifth Commandment admonishing believers to honor their parents, Winthrop curtly replied. She had violated the Commandment, he claimed, by aiding and encouraging the pro-Wheelwright petitioners, men who, by their words and actions, had "dishonored" the colony's "fathers"—its church and government officials. While Hutchinson admitted to having "entertained" Wheelwright and many of the petitioners in her home on numerous occasions, she strongly denied having conspired with them against the colony's rulers. Thoroughly frustrated by Anne's unwillingness to admit she had done anything wrong, Winthrop abruptly ended his first line of questioning by declaring that the magistrates knew full well she had aided the petitioners and had no intention of wasting any more of their time arguing "with those of your sex."

Moving on to the issue of Anne's meetings, Winthrop asserted that for Hutchinson to give spiritual instruction to men as well as large groups of females, as she had been doing in her home, was not in keeping with biblical teachings on the proper role of women in

EXCERPTS FROM THE TRANSCRIPT OF THE CIVIL TRIAL OF ANNE HUTCHINSON

The transcript of Anne Hutchinson's civil trial in November 1637 was first published in 1767, as part of a three-volume history of the Bay colony by Anne's great-great-grandson Thomas Hutchinson, Massachusetts' royal governor from 1771 to 1774. The following excerpts from the trial transcript are from the final stages of the hearing, when Anne shocked the court by claiming to have received "immediate revelations" from the Holy Spirit and Governor John Winthrop pronounced the sentence of banishment upon her.

> Mrs. Anne Hutchinson: If you please to give me leave I shall give you the ground of what I know to be true. . . . I bless the Lord, he hath let me see which was the clear ministry and which the wrong.
> Since that time I confess I have been more choice and he hath left me to distinguish between the voice of my beloved [Jesus Christ] and the voice of . . . antichrist. . . . Now if you do condemn me for speaking what in my conscience I know to be truth I must commit myself unto the Lord.
> Mr. Nowel (assistant to the court): How do you know that was the spirit?
> Mrs. Anne Hutchinson: How did Abraham know that it was God that bid him offer his son, being a breach of the sixth commandment?
> Deputy Governor Thomas Dudley: By an immediate voice.

religious matters. In common with "most men of his time," writes historian Francis Bremer, Winthrop "would not accept a woman publicly correcting or seeking to instruct a man." Anne immediately shot

Mrs. Anne Hutchinson: So to me by an immediate revelation.

Deputy Governor Thomas Dudley: How! an immediate revelation.

Mrs. Anne Hutchinson: By the voice of his own spirit to my soul. . . . You have power over my body but the Lord Jesus hath power over my body and soul; and assure yourselves thus much, you do as much as in you lies to put the Lord Jesus Christ from you, and if you go on in this course you begin, you will bring a curse upon you and your posterity, and the mouth of the Lord hath spoken it.

. . .

Governor John Winthrop: The court hath already declared themselves satisfied concerning the things you hear, and concerning the troublesomeness of her spirit and the danger of her course amongst us, which is not to be suffered. Therefore if it be the mind of the court that Mrs. Hutchinson for these things that appear before us is unfit for our society, and if it be the mind of the court that she shall be banished out of our liberties and imprisoned till she be sent away, let them hold up their hands. . . .

Governor John Winthrop: Mrs. Hutchinson, the sentence of the court you hear is that you are banished from out of our jurisdiction as being a woman not fit for our society, and are to be imprisoned till the court shall send you away.

back at Winthrop by quoting two biblical passages, one from Titus, which urged older women to teach younger women, and the other from the Book of Acts, which described a devout woman providing spiritual instruction to a newly converted male Christian. Once again unable to get Anne to acknowledge any wrongdoing on her part, the court proceeded to address the last and most serious of the various accusations against her: that she had "traduced" (slandered) the ministers and their preaching.

"SAY NO MORE"

It soon became clear to Anne that the foundation for the last charge against her was the meeting she had attended at John Cotton's house along with 10 prominent Massachusetts ministers almost exactly one year earlier. Under close questioning, Hutchinson all but admitted to having said at the meeting that, except for Cotton, none of the clergy were "able ministers of the New Testament." Nonetheless, she insisted, since the remark was made during the course of a private conversation, it should not be used as evidence that she had slandered the colony's ministers. Hutchinson's public-private distinction failed to impress Winthrop, however. In adjourning the trial until the next morning, he noted that the court had struggled unsuccessfully to make Hutchinson acknowledge "the error of [her] ways." He strongly urged her to spend the night reflecting on her misdeeds.

The next morning, to Winthrop's dismay, instead of returning to court humbled and repentant after a night of pondering her failings, Hutchinson came back more defiant than ever. First, she insisted that all the ministers who testified against her be compelled to swear their accounts under oath in keeping with English judicial practice. Then, she demanded that her spiritual mentor, John Cotton, be called as a defense witness. Cotton's less-than-forceful testimony on her behalf must have disappointed Hutchinson, however. Cotton testified that he could not recall Hutchinson saying anything that he considered to be slanderous about the colony's clergy at the meeting, but he also admitted that there were many gaps in his memories of that day.

"Perhaps now realizing that a conviction was inevitable, Hutchinson made a critical decision," writes Michael Winship. Convinced she had nothing to lose, she decided to share her personal spiritual vision with her prosecutors and judges. "I shall give you the ground [basis] of what I know to be true," she informed the court, although she was aware that the magistrates might "condemn" her for speaking her "conscience." By bringing her attention to certain biblical passages, she declared, God had revealed to her the "unfaithfulness of the churches, and the danger of them. . . ." Then, she said, God had shown her through an "immediate revelation"—a direct message from the Holy Spirit to her soul as opposed to one transmitted through a scriptural verse—how to discern between "which was the clear [correct] ministry and which the wrong." Another "immediate revelation" from the Holy Spirit had assured her that, although she would suffer persecution for her beliefs, God would safely deliver her from her enemies. Finally, she boldly proclaimed that the Holy Spirit had revealed to her that if the General Court and the rest of the colony's leadership continued along their corrupt spiritual path, "you will bring a curse upon you and your posterity [descendants], and the mouth of the Lord hath spoken it."

Anne Hutchinson's listeners in the Cambridge meetinghouse were shocked by her impassioned outburst. Not only had she had the audacity to threaten the governor and the rest of the court openly, but she had claimed that God had spoken to her directly through "immediate revelations" on at least three occasions. Orthodox Puritans believed that God had not spoken directly to people since biblical times. Consequently, Winthrop and most of his fellow court members could only conclude that Hutchinson must be "self-, and probably satanically, deluded," contends Michael Winship. The entire court, except for two deputies from Boston and one member who abstained from voting, raised their hands when Winthrop asked whether Hutchinson should be banished from

Massachusetts Bay on charges of slandering the ministers and for her seditious final speech. Seemingly unmoved by the harsh punishment the court had meted out to her, Anne remained recklessly defiant to the very end. "I desire to know wherefore I am banished," she demanded after Winthrop formally pronounced the sentence of banishment on her. "Say no more," the governor snapped, "the court knows wherefore and is satisfied."

8

Excommunication

Following her sentencing by the General Court on November 8, 1637, Anne Hutchinson was placed in the custody of court deputy Joseph Weld, the brother of the Reverend Thomas Weld, one of Anne's fiercest critics. Hutchinson was to remain under strict house arrest in Weld's home in Roxbury, several miles from Boston, until the arrival of spring permitted her to depart the colony. By placing her with Weld, Governor John Winthrop clearly hoped to isolate Anne from her followers, the vast majority of whom lived in Boston. To his dismay, however, Winthrop soon began to hear rumors that Hutchinson had been developing increasingly radical religious views during her detainment, and that her heretical ideas had somehow been making their way back to Boston.

In response to these unsettling reports, delegations of ministers began calling on Anne in Joseph Weld's home several times a week. Among the most frequent of her visitors were three particularly zealous orthodox preachers: Thomas Shephard of Cambridge, Hugh Peter of Salem, and Thomas Weld of Roxbury. During the course of their visits, Hutchinson supposedly admitted that she had come to question a number of mainstream Puritan teachings aside from the doctrines of preparation and sanctification. By early March, the clergymen had compiled a list of 29 theological errors that they suspected Anne of holding. Given the stunning breadth of her alleged heresies, just convicting Hutchinson of sedition in a civil court was not enough, the ministers concluded. Before she left Massachusetts forever in the spring, they decided, Hutchinson must be formally excommunicated (ejected) from the Boston church she had attended since coming to the colony 3½ years earlier.

"YOU HAVE STEPPED OUT OF YOUR PLACE"

Anne Hutchinson arrived at her old Boston meetinghouse for her excommunication hearing before the clergy and members of the First Church on the morning of March 15, 1638. Just a short time before, she could have counted on the loyal backing of a majority of her fellow church members. During the four months since Anne's civil trial, however, most of her followers had either returned to the orthodox camp or left the colony altogether. A week before the hearing, William Hutchinson, accompanied by more than a dozen of Anne's male disciples and their families, had departed Massachusetts Bay for what is today the state of Rhode Island. William and the others planned to build a new settlement on Aquidneck Island in Narragansett Bay. Anne was to join them there at the end of March, the date by which the General Court wanted her out of Massachusetts for good. Hutchinson, William Coddington, and several other members of the group had purchased the island from a Native American tribe with the help of Roger Williams, former minister of Salem's Puritan church and the founder of Providence Plantation, Rhode Island's first English settlement. Williams himself had been banished from Massachusetts Bay by the General Court in 1635 for spreading "new and dangerous opinions," including religious tolerance and the duty of the English settlers to reimburse New England's Native American inhabitants for the land the colonists lived on and farmed.

Like her civil trial, Anne Hutchinson's trial at the First Church of Boston dragged on for nearly two full days. For hours on end, Anne and her clerical prosecutors debated her nearly 30 purported theological errors, with Hutchinson displaying the same sharp intelligence, deep knowledge of the Bible, and indomitable spirit she had shown in defending herself before the magistrates of the General Court. When it was all over, Anne, who steadfastly denied all the charges alleged against her, was excommunicated more for her defiant attitude and what her critics viewed as her "haughty" pride than for any clearly definable heresy. As the case of the Reverend John Wheelwright aptly illustrates, Massachusetts' orthodox rulers had little patience with anyone, even a fellow minister, who dared to challenge their authority. For a woman to do so, however, was particularly galling. According both to the orthodox rulers' interpretation of the Bible and longstanding cultural traditions, women were supposed to be meek and submissive rather than assertive, opinionated, and self-assured like Anne. Toward the end of Anne's excommunication hearing, writes Selma Williams, Hugh Peter "incisively cut to the heart of the ministers' quarrel with Anne" when he scolded her for not knowing her proper place in the church and Puritan society in general. "I would commend this to your consideration," accused the Salem minister, "that you have stepped out of your place, you have rather been a husband than a wife, a preacher than a hearer, and a magistrate than a subject, and so you have thought to carry

After Hutchinson was excommunicated from the Boston church, one of her greatest supporters, Mary Dyer, followed her out of the meetinghouse in a show of loyalty. Dyer later became a Quaker, a religion that allowed her and other women to take on leadership roles. Dyer was executed in 1660 (*above*) for refusing to leave Massachusetts.

all things in church and commonwealth as you would, and have not been humbled."

Shortly after Peter's tirade against Anne, Hutchinson's old enemy, the Reverend John Wilson, formally expelled her from the First Church. Clearly savoring his revenge, Wilson proclaimed: "In the name of our Lord Jesus Christ and in the name of the church, I do not only pronounce you worthy to be cast out, but I cast you out! And in the name of Christ, I do deliver you up to Satan that you may learn no more to blaspheme, to seduce, and to lie! Therefore, I command you in the name of this church as a leper *to withdraw yourself out of the congregation!*" As Anne rose from her bench to leave, her friend and follower Mary Dyer also rose and accompanied her down the aisle toward the church door. Dyer's very public show of support for Anne took courage. Again and again during the excommunication hearing, Anne's judges, including even her onetime idol, John Cotton, had warned the females in the audience in the strongest possible terms to shun Hutchinson and her "corrupting" spiritual and moral influence. Determined to have the last word, when Anne reached the door, she turned back to face her accusers. "The Lord judgeth not as man judgeth. Better to be cast out of the church than to deny Christ," she declared in a loud, clear voice. Then, hand-in-hand with Mary Dyer, she walked out of the Boston meetinghouse for the final time.

EXILE AND DEATH

Within days of her excommunication from the First Church, Anne Hutchinson and her six youngest children departed Massachusetts Bay for the settlement her husband and supporters had founded in Rhode Island. At some point after completing the arduous, six-day journey from Boston to Aquidneck Island, Anne suffered a painful miscarriage. Rumors that the 46-year-old "heretic" had delivered more than two dozen separate masses of lifeless tissue soon reached Winthrop back in Boston. The governor immediately discerned God's hand at work in the unusual miscarriage. Anne's "monstrous" multiple birth symbolized her many "monstrous heresies," Winthrop asserted, exulting in his diary how perfectly "the wisdom of God fitted this judgment to her sin."

MARY DYER

Anne Hutchinson's close friend and supporter Mary Barrett Dyer was born in England around 1610 and married William Dyer, a well-to-do London Puritan, in 1633. Two years later, the couple migrated to Boston, where they were soon admitted to the First Church. John Winthrop described her in his diary as "a very proper and fair [attractive] woman" although "of a very proud spirit, and much addicted to revelations."

Both she and her husband attended Anne Hutchinson's religious meetings, and, after Anne was banished, they followed her to Aquidneck Island.

After Hutchinson's death, the Dyers moved back to England for a time, where Mary converted to the Religious Society of Friends, better known as Quakerism. Quakers emphasized the believer's inward religious experience, preaching that doctrines and traditional churches hindered true faith. Quakers were also quite progressive in their ideas regarding women's proper religious roles,

Little is known with certainty about Anne Hutchinson's years in Rhode Island. According to most accounts, soon after settling on Aquidneck Island, Hutchinson returned to her controversial practice of leading religious meetings for men as well as women in her home. She also launched "what amounted to a guerilla holy war" against her former Boston church, notes Michael Winship, firing off a series of belligerent letters to the congregation in which she predicted that God's wrath would fall on Massachusetts Bay and its erring Puritan churches. In response to Anne's disturbing letters, the clergy and elders of the First Church sent a small delegation to Aquidneck in 1640 to try to convince Hutchinson of her theological errors one last time and bring her back to the "true" faith. It quickly became clear to the delegates, however, that Anne allowing female preachers from the founding of the Religious Society of Friends in England in the early 1650s. Mary returned to New England in 1658, the same year that the Massachusetts General Court passed a harsh law banning Quakers from the colony under pain of death. In October 1659, Dyer was sentenced to hang in Boston, along with two male Quaker friends, after the three dissenters defied a court order to leave the Bay Colony for good. At the last minute, Governor John Endicott stayed Dyer's execution and officially banished her from Massachusetts again. Undaunted, a little more than six months later Dyer was back in the colony to protest its repressive anti-Quaker policies. Once again Dyer was sentenced to hang, but this time the execution was actually carried out. The hanging of the middle-aged mother of six on Boston Common on June 1, 1660, so shocked the people of Massachusetts that executions of Quakers in the colony stopped following Dyer's death, although members of the sect continued to be banned from Massachusetts.

had no interest whatsoever in returning to the orthodox fold. Indeed, according to the delegation's official report, at one point she even went so far as to denounce her former church as "the Whore and Strumpet of Boston." The delegation was horrified by what they considered as Anne's unchristian—and decidedly unladylike—outburst, but William backed his free-spoken spouse unreservedly, informing the delegates that he was "more nearly tied to his wife than to the church, he thought her to be a dear saint and servant of God."

In 1642, Anne suffered a devastating personal blow when her beloved husband of 30 years died at the age of 55. Soon after William Hutchinson's death, Anne resolved to leave Rhode Island for the Dutch colony of New Netherland in present-day New York. Her decision to move to New Amsterdam seems to have been rooted in rumors then circulating in Rhode Island that Massachusetts Bay was planning to take over the entire Narragansett Bay region, including Aquidneck Island. Reportedly as the result of a scriptural revelation, Anne decided to settle with her six youngest children and three other families from the Aquidneck community near Pelham Bay, in what is today the borough of the Bronx in New York City.

As it turned out, Anne's new home was located in the middle of territory inhabited by the Wecquaesgeek band of Indians, who had been involved in a bloody war with the Dutch since 1640. Although warned by the Wecquaesgeek to move elsewhere, Anne, confident of divine protection, stayed put. In August of 1643, Wecquaesgeek warriors raided her farm, murdering and scalping Anne, five of her six children, and most members of the three families that had accompanied the Hutchinsons to New Amsterdam barely a year earlier. Only Anne's youngest daughter, 9-year-old Susan, survived the attack. Taken captive by the Wecquaesgeeks, she spent nearly a decade with her captors before being ransomed and sent to live with relatives in Boston.

When news of the murder of Anne and her five children reached Boston, Hutchinson's orthodox critics interpreted the killings as a sign of God's displeasure with her. Thomas Weld asserted that he had "never heard that the Indians in those parts did ever before this commit the like outrage upon any one family, and therefore God's hand is the more apparently seen herein, to pick out this woeful woman, to make her and those belonging to her an unheard-of heavy example of their cruelty above all others." John Winthrop agreed with Weld wholeheartedly, comparing Hutchinson's slaying to the bloody demise of the notorious biblical villainess Jezebel. A Phoenician by birth, Jezebel was the scheming and headstrong wife of Ahab, the Hebrew king of Israel. After Jezebel tried to lead her subjects into the worship of pagan idols and away from the one

ANNE AND WILLIAM HUTCHINSON'S CHILDREN

Between 1613 and 1636, Anne Hutchinson gave birth to 15 children, all of whom were born in England except the last, Zuriel, who was born in Massachusetts Bay. The Hutchinson children's baptismal dates are listed below; their birth dates were probably two to three days earlier.

Edward	June 28, 1613
Susanna	September 4, 1614
Richard	January 8, 1616
Faith	August 14, 1617
Bridget	January 15, 1619
Francis	December 24, 1620
Elizabeth	February 17, 1622
William	June 22, 1623
Samuel	December 17, 1624
Anne	May 5, 1626[*]
Mary	February 22, 1628[*]
Katherine	February 7, 1630[*]
William	September 28, 1631[*] (named for his deceased older brother)
Susan	November 15, 1633
Zuriel	March 13, 1636[*]

[*]Anne, Mary, Katherine, William, and Zuriel were killed with their mother in August 1643 near Pelham Bay, New York, during an Indian raid.

"true" God, Jehovah, her chief Hebrew opponent, Jehu, trampled Jezebel to death beneath the hooves of his horse and left her corpse for the dogs to eat.

Native American warriors of the Wecquaesgeek band killed and scalped Hutchinson and five of her children. Leaders of the Boston church smugly explained her death as God punishing the wicked. John Winthrop compared her murder to the bloody slaying of biblical villainess Jezebel.

ANNE HUTCHINSON'S LEGACY

After her death, "Anne Hutchinson's personal influence proved ephemeral [short-lived]," writes Michael Winship. According to Winship, most of her disciples either perished with her at Pelham Bay or were drawn into the Quaker sect, a non-Calvinist Protestant movement that first arrived in New England from Britain in the mid-1650s. Hutchinson's fame as colonial America's first female religious leader increased considerably following her murder, however, primarily due to the efforts of her archenemy, John Winthrop. In early 1644, Winthrop published a hostile account of Anne's civil and church trials titled *A Short Story Of The Rise, Reign, And Ruin Of The Antinomians, Familists, and Libertines*. The governor's tract was meant both to justify the Massachusetts authorities' harsh treatment of Anne and to warn English Puritans against her "dangerous" theological opinions, particularly her alleged Antinomianism. His negative portrayal of Anne in the *Short Story* as the haughty, deceitful ringleader of a heretical faction bent on destroying New England's churches went through numerous editions and remained the standard account of Hutchinson for more than a century. Finally, during the 1760s, Anne's great-great-grandson Thomas Hutchinson included a previously unpublished eyewitness transcript of her civil trial in his history of Massachusetts that placed Anne in a more sympathetic light. Instead of the manipulative and self-aggrandizing "American Jezebel" whom Winthrop had portrayed in his *Short Story,* the Anne Hutchinson depicted in the trial transcript came across as courageously honest and genuinely devout.

Over the course of the past 2½ centuries since the transcript of her trial before the General Court was first published, Anne Hutchinson has attained near legendary status. Nineteenth- and early twentieth-century commentators praised her as an early champion of religious freedom, and as the feminist movement took hold in the United States during the late 1900s, she was held up as a pioneer for women's rights. Today, both of these views regarding Hutchinson and her legacy have been largely discredited. Far from being a champion of religious liberty, Anne was every bit as intolerant of the spiritual beliefs of the orthodox Puritan preachers whose preaching she attacked as they were of her beliefs, most scholars now agree. Most also concur that, although Hutchinson clearly stepped out of traditional gender roles in her religious activities and bold courtroom performance, her powerful spiritual convictions, rather than a desire to advance the overall position of women in Puritan society, were the driving force behind her defiant actions and words.

Yet, whether Anne Hutchinson may accurately be seen as either a pioneering feminist or a champion of religious freedom, as she has often been labeled in the past, her place in American history is assured. Hutchinson was not afraid to speak up for her beliefs or assume a leadership role in a society that frowned on all challenges to the established order and refused to allow females, even if highly educated and principled, to wield public power. Today, nearly 400 years after she was banished from the Massachusetts Bay Colony, the issues raised by her life and career—gender equality, freedom of speech, respect for the religious practices and beliefs of others, and the proper relationship between church and government—still resonate.

Chronology

1591	Anne Marbury is born in Alford, England, around July 17 or 18.
1603	Queen Elizabeth I dies and James I becomes king of England.
1605	Francis Marbury moves his family to London after being appointed vicar of St. Martin in the Vintry parish.
1611	Death of Francis Marbury.
1612	Anne marries William Hutchinson and returns to Alford.
1613	Anne gives birth to the first of her 15 children, Edward.
1620	Separatist Puritans (the Pilgrims) found America's first permanent Puritan settlement at Plymouth.
1625	James I dies and Charles I becomes king of England.
1630	Two of Anne's daughters die, probably from the bubonic plague.

1630	Nearly 1,000 Puritans leave England for the Massachusetts Bay Colony under John Winthrop.
1633	The Reverend John Cotton flees England for Massachusetts Bay.
1634	Hutchinson family emigrates to Massachusetts Bay.
1635	Anne starts holding weekly religious discussions for women in her home.
1636	Anne's meetings attract males as well as females and her teachings become increasingly controversial.
	Henry Vane is elected governor of Massachusetts.

TIMELINE

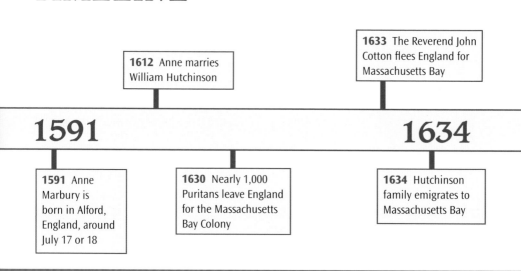

1612 Anne marries William Hutchinson

1633 The Reverend John Cotton flees England for Massachusetts Bay

1591

1634

1591 Anne Marbury is born in Alford, England, around July 17 or 18

1630 Nearly 1,000 Puritans leave England for the Massachusetts Bay Colony

1634 Hutchinson family emigrates to Massachusetts Bay

1637	John Winthrop defeats Vane to become governor of Massachusetts.
	Anne is convicted of heresy by the General Court and is sentenced to banishment.
1638	First Church of Boston tries and excommunicates Anne.
	Anne leaves Massachusetts Bay for exile in Rhode Island.
1642	Husband William Hutchinson dies.
	Anne and her younger children move to the Dutch colony of New Amsterdam.
1643	Anne and five of her children are killed by Native Americans near Pelham Bay, New York.

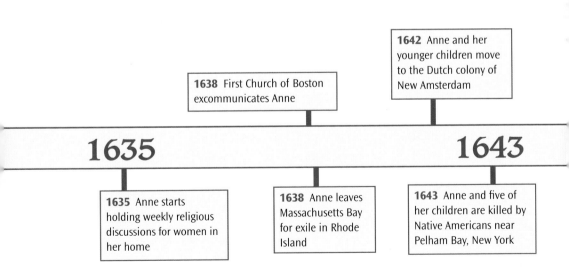

1642 Anne and her younger children move to the Dutch colony of New Amsterdam

1638 First Church of Boston excommunicates Anne

1635

1643

1635 Anne starts holding weekly religious discussions for women in her home

1638 Anne leaves Massachusetts Bay for exile in Rhode Island

1643 Anne and five of her children are killed by Native Americans near Pelham Bay, New York

Bibliography

Battis, Emery. *Saints and Sectaries: Anne Hutchinson and the Antinomian Controversy in the Massachusetts Bay Colony.* Chapel Hill: University of North Carolina Press, 1962.

Bremer, Francis J. *John Winthrop: America's Forgotten Founding Father.* New York: Oxford University Press, 2003.

Bremer, Francis J. *The Puritan Experiment: New England Society from Bradford to Edwards.* New York; St. Martin's Press, 1976.

Hall, David. *The Antinomian Controversy, 1636–1638: A Documentary History.* Middletown, CT: Wesleyan University Press, 1968.

LaPlante, Eve. *American Jezebel: The Uncommon Life of Anne Hutchinson, the Woman Who Defied the Puritans.* San Francisco: Harper San Francisco, 2004.

Smith, Cheryl C. "Out of Her Place: Anne Hutchinson and the Dislocation of Power in New World Politics." *Journal of American Culture* 29 (2006): 437–453.

Westerkamp, Marilyn. "Anne Hutchinson, the Puritan Patriarchs, and the Power of the Spirit." In *The Human Tradition in America from the Colonial Era Through Reconstruction,* edited by Charles W. Calhoun. Wilmington, Del.: Scholarly Resources, 2002, pp. 17–38.

Williams, Selma. *Divine Rebel: The Life of Anne Marbury Hutchinson.* New York: Holt Rinehart and Winston, 1981.

Winship, Michael P. *The Times And Trials Of Anne Hutchinson: Puritans Divided.* Lawrence: University Press of Kansas, 2005.

Further Resources

BOOKS

Butler, Jon. *Religion in Colonial America*. New York: Oxford University Press, 2000.

Collier, Christopher, and James Lincoln Collier. *Pilgrims and Puritans, 1620–1676*. New York: Marshall Cavendish, 1998.

Crawford, Deborah. *Four Women in a Violent Time*. New York: Crown, 1970.

Ilgenfritz, Elizabeth. *Anne Hutchinson*. New York: Chelsea House, 1991.

Slavicek, Louise Chipley. *Life Among the Puritans*. San Diego: Lucent Books, 2001.

WEB SITES

Mass Moments: Anne Hutchinson Banished, March 22, 1638
http://www.massmoments.org/moment.cfm?mid=88

Mrs. Anne Hutchinson—Trial at the Court at Newton. 1637
http://www.piney-2.com/ColAnnHutchTrial.html

Puritanism in New England
http://www.wsu.edu/~campbelld/amlit/purdef.htm

Picture Credits

PAGE

Index

Page numbers in *italics* indicate photos or illustrations.

A

Alford 12–13, 26–29, *28*, 32–33, 35
Anglican Church (Church of England)
   commitment to reform 59, 61–62, *62*
   Francis Marbury and 16–19
   history of 13–17
   John Cotton and 37
   lay ministers and 34
   salvation and 54
   shortage of ministers in 21–22
annulments 14
Antinomianism 82, 107
Aquidneck Island 98–99, 101–102
Arbella sermon 61–63
Aspinwall, William 76, 88
Aylmer, John 17–18, 21

B

banishment 9, 9–10, 88, 95–96, 99, 103
baptisms 29
Bible 16, 21, *23*, 50–51
birth of Anne Hutchinson 12
bishops, promotion of 17–18
Black Death 48–50
blasphemy 77
Boleyn, Anne 14, *15*
Book of Martyrs (Fox) 21, *23*
Boston 67–72. *See also* Massachusetts Bay Colony

Bradstreet, Anne 30–31
Bradstreet, Simon 30–31
bubonic plague 48–50

C

Calvin, John 41, 42, *43*
Calvinism *43*
Cambridge University 37
Catherine of Aragon 14, *15*
Catholic Church 14, 16
Charles I (king of England) 55–56, 59
charters 59
childbirth 29–31. *See also* Midwifes
children 26–27, 47, 65–66, 101, 104–105, *106*
church membership 67–69, *70*
Church of England. *See* Anglican Church
"city on a hill" sermon 77
Clement VII (pope) 14, *15*
Coddington, William 76, 98–99
Coggeshall, John 76, 88
Cotton, John
   in Alford 35–39, *36*
   as defense witness 95–96
   departure of to New World 58–63
   First Church of Boston and 68–69, 73
   John Laud and 55–58
   ministers conference and 81–83
   revelation and 50
   salvation and 45–46, 53–54
Cotton, Sarah 63

About the Author

Louise Chipley Slavicek received her master's degree in history from the University of Connecticut. She is the author of numerous articles on American and world history for scholarly journals and for young people's magazines, including *Highlights for Children, Cobblestone,* and *Calliope*. Her more than two dozen books for young people include *Life Among the Puritans, Women of the American Revolution, Annie Montague Alexander,* and *Women and the Civil War*. She lives in Ohio with her husband, Jim, a research biologist, and their two children, Krista and Nathan.